MARK A. BROUGHTON-TAYLOR

49 LORDSWOOD RD.,
HARBORNE
BIRMINGHAM B17 9QT

☆ *Quick Skits*
& Discussion
Starters

by
Chuck Bolte and Paul McCusker

Group Books

Loveland, Colorado

Quick Skits & Discussion Starters

Credits
Edited by Nancy M. Shaw
Cover and book design by Judy Atwood
Cover illustration by Jean Bruns

ISBN 0-931529-68-9

Printed in the United States of America

Acknowledgments

A collection of warm-ups and sketches as found in this book aren't generally written in a concentrated period of time—at least, not for us. We assembled this collection over a long period—involving a variety of people and different sources of inspiration.

First, we must thank our wives (Soozi and Elizabeth, in case you were wondering) not only for demeaning themselves enough to marry us, but because they'd kill us if we let another book go by without some sort of acknowledgment.

Again, our thanks to Jim Custer, Bob Hoose and the Jeremiah People. Heartfelt gratitude to Calvary Community Church in Thousand Oaks, California, and the gang in "Apple Corps." Deep appreciation to Cindy Hansen and the wonderful crew at Group Publishing. And where would we be without the many talented folks at Grace Baptist Church in Bowie, Maryland? (It's a rhetorical question.)

If we should have said "thanks" to you and didn't, feel free to write your name here: _____.

And last, but not least, our thankfulness for mutual friendship.

CONTENTS

Sketches

Introduction

If you're familiar with *Youth Ministry Drama & Comedy (Better Than Bathrobes but Not Quite Broadway)* written by yours trulies, then you already know our feelings about the use of drama and comedy in the church. (If you're not familiar with it, then we hope you feel sufficiently guilty to buy a copy.) Simply put, drama and comedy can supplement and enhance nearly every program your church can come up with.

Yes, that includes youth meetings.

And why not? Where better than a youth meeting will actions speak louder than words? Few young people enjoy sitting and listening to someone talk for an hour, but let them *do* something—let them *see* something—and they'll not only get involved, but they'll leave feeling they've learned a few things (without intending to).

That's the purpose of this book—to give you practical tools for "breaking the ice," "bashing the boredom," "opening minds" and "reaching hearts" (or any other expressions you might want to throw in).

It's easy. Well, reasonably easy. First you'll find a variety of warm-ups to help group members get involved. These exercises provide opportunities for kids to interact with one another and enhance their communication skills. Browse through the warm-ups, and use them with or without the sketches, depending on what you've planned for that particular meeting. Don't be surprised if you find uses for these exercises outside the suggestions in this book.

Beyond the warm-ups, you'll notice a variety of sketches (or skits, as some would call them). Each is headed by a topic that identifies the theme of the sketch and helps you choose the most appropriate sketch for your meeting. (All right, all right, so we got the idea from various hymnbooks. We never claimed our ideas were completely original.)

Following the topic is the title of the sketch and a preparation section that suggests which warm-ups to use and what people and resources you'll need to put the sketch together. To your delight, you'll find that most sketches will prove easy to do. We did this on purpose. Group members can read the sketch "cold," as in a readers theater. Or some group members could do impromptu acting while someone else reads the script. Or if your group members are ambitious, they can prepare the sketches a week or two in advance (including rehearsals and line memorization). It's entirely up to you.

After each sketch, we've assembled discussion questions that help individuals pry into their deeper feelings and hopefully make them think about things they might otherwise ignore. (They sure made us think.) Of course, the goal is to help young people raise their sights beyond everyday experiences to the spiritual truths at the heart of every problem and solution; then ultimately turn those truths into action.

We won't pretend these warm-ups and sketches won't require some effort. They will. But if you didn't put in a little effort, you wouldn't have a youth group, at least not for long. As we said already: Actions speak louder than words.

And, oh yeah . . . don't forget to have fun!

Warm-Ups

Warm-Ups

If you skipped over the unbelievably articulate introduction to this book, you're probably wondering: "What in the world are warm-ups? And what do they have to do with anything?" Warm-ups are exercises that help your group members develop strong dramatic, creative and communicative skills. These exercises are critical for establishing a creative, open atmosphere. Exercises attempt to involve all group members—regardless of personality, race, color, creed and make of clothing. And if we may state the obvious, *all group members* means *you* too.

Use the exercises alone or with the sketches in the second half of this book beginning on page 31. Specific warm-ups are suggested at the beginning of each sketch, but don't always expect a direct correlation between the two. We did that on purpose. Trust us.

☆1. Emphasis

This exercise helps your youth group members realize there's more than one way to say something. It also demonstrates that if something is said the wrong way, the statement can mean something completely different than was originally intended. This fun exercise illustrates how a simple change of emphasis can change the entire meaning of a sentence. It also demonstrates how attitude, voice volume and facial expressions dramatically affect how someone hears what is said. Read the following example emphasizing the underlined word:

<u>Why</u> don't you go to bed?

Why <u>don't</u> you go to bed?

Why don't <u>you</u> go to bed?

Why don't you go to <u>bed</u>?

Try some of these sentences. Ask that kids read each sentence with a minimum of four different emphases.

● You go down to see it.
● If you could just see her.
● Just take a moment and think.
● This could be the most beautiful thing yet.
● When do you expect the train to arrive?
● This is going to be phenomenal!
● Why can't you see her face?

Now have group members each make up their own sentences and do the same exercise. Be certain they add at least four varying emotions to their delivery for maximum effectiveness.

☆2. Gobbledygook

This exercise is a twist on the previous idea. Ask two or three youth group members to carry on a conversation in gibberish (nonsensical, non-existent words made up on the spur of the moment). But the conversation should sound as if it makes perfect sense to those doing the talking. In essence, it should sound as if we're listening to a conversation in a foreign language. This should help your group members develop the ability to think on their feet and make real what isn't.

☆3. Lies

Ask for five volunteers from your youth group. Take them outside the meeting room and briefly explain the following exercise. Instruct each person to think of the most unusual experience he or she has ever had. It doesn't need to be anything spectacular. As a matter of fact, it's often better if it isn't something out of the ordinary. Then ask one of the five to fabricate a story that isn't true but isn't out of the realm of possibility either. Encourage volunteers to keep their stories as brief and yet as detailed as possible.

When you re-enter the room, tell the group that you've asked these five individuals to share their most unusual experiences. Have group members listen closely to each story. After volunteers have told their tales, inform the group that one individual was lying. Ask group members to discuss the stories and identify the "liar."

After the liar is identified, ask another five (or fewer if you have a small group) to step outside. Give the same explanation, and choose one individual to be the liar. This time group members will listen with "different ears," and the dynamics of the situation should change.

Here's another variation of this exercise: Ask the liar in the first group to tell a serious imaginary story, such as describing the details and feelings behind the death of a relative. When you get to the end of the exercise, ask the following questions to generate discussion about attitudes toward people who lie.

● When I told you that one individual was lying, how did you feel?

● Why did you feel this way?

● Are there different "degrees" of lying?

● If so, where do you draw the line? Does that line change with every situation?

● What does the Bible say about lying? (Read Leviticus 19:11; Proverbs 6:16-19; 14:5; and Colossians 3:9.)

● How do these biblical statements about lying apply to our everyday relationships?

★4. Believe It or Not

Use this exercise creatively to "loosen up" your youth group. Before the meeting, round up 10 or more objects of varying sizes and shapes. Find unique objects, such as a kitchen whisk or a camera, that have an ordinary use and purpose. Don't limit yourself to inanimate objects. Using a group member as an object can offer a lot of fun. Set all objects on a table.

Ask different individuals from the group to choose one object and create a story around it. Stories can take any form. They can be based on an actual event or pure fantasy; they can be fun or serious. Even though kids may take three or four minutes to create their stories, this exercise promotes and hones creativity and encourages individuals to listen to one another.

★5. I Wish I'd Told You

Dim the lights in the meeting room so it's difficult to identify facial features. Then have a volunteer stand in front of the group. Have the individual turn his or her back to the group and focus on a spot on the floor. Ask the individual to imagine that he or she is standing next to a friend's or relative's graveside or coffin. Have the individual casually talk to that person as if he or she had been gone for a long time and needed to be updated on all that had happened.

After a minute or two, ask the volunteer to tell that person some of the things he or she never had the opportunity or never took the time to say when that person was alive.

Obviously, this exercise can create emotional vulnerability, and the leader must handle it with great sensitivity. Since most group members have experienced the death of a loved one (by such things as natural causes, car accidents, drowning, disease, suicide or drug overdoses), this time together can be a therapeutic experience.

☆6. Effecting Sound Effects

Purchase or borrow some sound-effects records. Choose a variety of sounds from different albums, or create your own sounds and record them on tape. (Note: Most sound-effect records contain only certain types of related sounds, such as the sounds of war—gunshots, people marching or a sergeant shouting orders.)

Make certain the sound effects you select don't last longer than 10 to 15 seconds. The general rule: the shorter the better but long enough to be identified. Choose sounds such as a gunshot, an egg frying, a car engine turning over but not starting, a clock ticking, an alarm going off, a person tap dancing, people laughing, a dog barking, cows mooing, a mountain stream gently flowing, a toilet flushing or a woman screaming. Obviously, there are hundreds of options.

Have group members form a circle. Ask for a volunteer to start the exercise. Have the volunteer react in an appropriate manner to the first sound effect. For example, if the sound is of marching soldiers, the volunteer could march around the circle. When that sound is finished, have the next person in the circle react to the next sound effect—and so on around the circle. So start the tape and have fun!

☆7. Musical Imagination

Prior to the meeting, set up a videocassette recorder and a TV monitor. Rent various movie tapes. Select musical excerpts from the tapes, some of your favorites and some from the more obscure motion pictures.

At the meeting ask group members to close their eyes, then play one of the selections. When each selection is finished, have people open their eyes and describe what images came to their minds. Some individuals may identify the movie scene. Others may develop stories around their impressions. After a brief discussion, replay the scene.

Use films with particularly visual scores such as *Out of Africa*; *The Mission*; *Jaws*; *Silverado*; *E.T., The Extra-Terrestrial*; *Doctor Zhivago* and *Raiders of the Lost Ark*. You might also choose musicals such as *The Sound of Music* or Disney films such as *The Aristocats*, along with others you're familiar with.

Take this exercise further by playing heavy metal or pop music videos that haven't originated from films. After playing those particular pieces, ask group members to describe their feelings. Then discuss the contrasting emotional reactions to various musical forms. Talk about the influence music has on our everyday lives. For example, how does what you're listening to prior to going to school affect your attitude during the first few hours of that day? Or how does the music you listen to affect your relationships with people of the opposite sex?

★8. Story Mime

This simple and fun exercise will help your group members develop observational skills. Arrange chairs in a large circle allowing space between chairs for individuals to move. Ask group members to stand. Inform them that you're about to take them through an average day—from the time they get up until they finally go to bed. Explain that they're going to re-enact *everything* you describe exactly as they would do it every day. Every action should look real and be consistent with how each individual would carry out the action you describe. Here are two sample scripts you can use. Actions to be mimed appear in italics. When you read the italicized directions, allow time for group members to complete their actions.

Story 1

You got up early in the morning, just as you do every school morning. *Turn off your alarm and walk to the shower. Pick up a towel and dry off. Wrap the towel around you. Return to your bedroom* where your clothes are laid out. In front of you is a shirt, a pair of pants, a belt, socks and a pair of shoes. *Put your clothes on.*

After you're dressed, *walk to the kitchen* where a box of cereal along with a carton of milk awaits you. *Get a bowl from the cabinet and a spoon from the drawer. Sit down at the table. Open the box and pour some cereal into the bowl. Add milk and eat it.* Make us believe that this cereal tastes slightly better than the box it came in. When finished, *peel an orange and eat it. Return to the bathroom, pick up your toothbrush and toothpaste and brush your teeth.*

Before leaving the house, *put on your coat and check out your image in the mirror.* You look great. *Rush to school. Approach the building with hesitancy. Indicate that you've just realized why no one's here.* It's Saturday.

Story 2

You're on a camping trip. You just woke up from a night in the tent with your brother who snores like a gorilla. *Struggle out of your sleeping bag and climb out of the tent.* Someone else in your family has already fired up the camp stove. *Find a frying pan, a spatula and some eggs. Cook the eggs*—sunny side up. *Slide them onto a plate and eat them*—even if you don't like your eggs sunny side up. Now you're ready for the day.

Grab your backpack and fishing pole and hike to a nearby lake. As you walk along the path, *reach out to pick up an unusual stick.* It's a snake! *Run!* Having covered the two-mile trek in less than three minutes, *sit down and catch your breath.*

Now you're ready to go fishing. *Reach into the can of worms and place one on a hook.* Having terminally impaled this helpless creature, *cast your line into the water and wait patiently.* Suddenly, *you feel a tug on your line. Jerk your pole to set the hook, and begin reeling in an active fish. Pull it ashore. Take its massive eight-inch body off the hook and clean it.*

March proudly back to camp. As you walk, *help us realize that for the past two hours you've been sitting in poison ivy*—with a tear in the seat of your pants.

☆9. *Picture This*

Many words when spoken or read create instant mental images. Help your group verbally describe those images and challenge their creative thinking with this exercise. When using the following words, ask group members first to visualize and then describe what they see. Certain words will create clearer pictures for certain individuals. Encourage individuals to put themselves in their picture. Remind them not only to describe in detail what they see but also to identify what they're feeling. Use words that bring immediate pictures to mind such as:

ship	cliff	cake
castle	farm	snow
mountain	bridge	Mary
Jesus	dessert	race car
church	Apostle Paul	Joshua
fire	fish	river

Use the individuals' different description of the biblical characters as a springboard to discuss what the Bible says about the physical appearance of these individuals. What clues did people suggest that help us picture these biblical individuals in our minds? How do these mental images affect our view of those individuals? This exercise can be applied not only to biblical characters but also to biblical settings. Create your own list and have fun!

☆10. *Fractured Sayings*

Write the following list of famous sayings on newsprint so everyone can see them. Have group members create new sentences that include one of these sayings. The new "fractured sayings" can be either funny or serious. For example, to the familiar quote "How do I love thee? Let me count the ways," an individual might add, "Let's see; one, two, three . . ."

- I regret that I have but one life to give up for my country.
- 'Tis better to have loved and lost than never to have loved at all.
- Seek ye first the kingdom of God.
- I have not yet begun to fight.
- Put your money where your mouth is.
- Walk softly and carry a big stick.

● Take the log out of your own eye before you take the speck out of your brother's eye.

● Keep a stiff upper lip.

● Fight fire with fire.

● Christians aren't perfect, just forgiven.

● Christianity is more than a religion, it's a way of life.

● If you can't stand the heat, get out of the kitchen.

● The only way to have a friend is to be one.

☆11. *Living Pictures*

Bring to your meeting a number of interesting pictures or photographs, preferably those depicting some sort of action. Choose one of the pictures. Then ask group members to come to the front and assume the same positions and facial expressions of those in the picture. Have them "freeze" in that position.

Choose one of the individuals as a lead character. When you ask group members to "unfreeze," the lead character must start a conversation that seems consistent with what the picture appears to portray. Sometimes individuals involved in the "living picture" need an opportunity to discuss ahead of time what they think the picture's characters are talking about.

For even more fun, use an opaque projector to project a picture on the wall or have a photograph changed into a slide and project it on a screen next to those in the living picture. Adding props similar to those in the picture can add even more interest.

☆12. *In Between*

Prior to your meeting, choose a script or a portion of a script that's completely unfamiliar to the group. You can find usable scripts in the drama section of your local library. Or use scripts from our prior book *Youth Ministry Drama & Comedy* or any of the resources listed in this book. (See "Additional Resources.")

Once you've located an appropriate script, choose an interesting scene. Read part of the scene aloud to give an indication of who the characters are. Then go to the end of the scene and read the closing lines.

At this point assign characters to various group members, asking them to improvise, or make up, the middle portion of the script so the ending will make sense. A sample might look like this:

JOHN I can't believe you did it! I mean you actually did it!

JERRY Hey, I had to. There just weren't too many options.

JOHN Yeah, but to Jennifer? I mean, we're talking Jennifer!

JERRY Gimme a break, all I did was . . . *(Jennifer enters)* Oh, uh . . . hi, Jen . . .

JENNIFER Hi John. *(Looks serious)* Jerry, listen, about last night . . .

[Improvisation]

JOHN Boy, am I glad you two got that resolved.

JENNIFER Me too. I mean it wouldn't have been so bad if he'd just left it alone. But to talk about the rhinoceros that way is a bit too much.

☆13. *Body Language*

Write the following statements on strips of paper. Have volunteers choose a strip and use only facial expressions, hands, arms and legs to "speak" these thoughts. After each "body statement," ask group members to decide what was said. Unlike charades, clues for words, syllables and names aren't permitted.

- Get lost.
- I love you.
- Would you please help me?
- I don't understand.
- Why did you do that?
- I don't believe it.
- It wasn't my fault.
- Your feet stink.
- Your slip is showing.
- I'm scared.
- Don't pick it up.
- Would you go out with me?
- Call the police.
- Pass the ketchup.

Take this exercise one step further by having group members carry on entire conversations with one another in this fashion. They can use these statements or make up some of their own.

☆14. *Deceptive Faces*

Have various group members say the statements in Warm-Up 13 with facial expressions and vocal inflections that are *opposite* of the normal feeling behind the phrases. For example, with a smile on your face and a friendly tone in your voice, tell someone, "Get lost."

☆15. *Memories*

The week before this meeting, ask group members each to bring in one object from their childhood—a toy, blanket, book, photo or whatever. Have a show-and-tell time for kids to talk about these objects and what part they play in their childhood memories.

☆16. *Photo Feelings*

Prior to your meeting, take photographs and slides or clip magazine pictures that reflect people in various life situations and places. For example:

- a beautiful country scene
- a small child with a parent
- an inner-city ghetto
- a teenager with his or her pet
- a person walking by the ocean
- a policeman
- a starving child in Africa
- two people arguing on a sports playing field
- a bum on a park bench
- a teenager on a motorcycle, bike or skateboard
- a dead body
- a person hang gliding or windsurfing
- a war scene
- a teenager sleeping in a bed
- a janitor
- a family walking out of church
- someone crying
- a remote Indian tribe involved in a ritual
- a pastor preaching
- an executive leaning over a desk of papers
- teenagers throwing a ball or Frisbee in a park
- a young person eating something messy

● a prison scene containing at least one young person
(Don't limit yourself to these suggestions.)

Select 10 pictures that will elicit contrasting emotions such as a beautiful country scene and an inner-city ghetto. Number the pictures. Gather paper and a pencil for each group member.

When the meeting begins, pass out paper and pencils. Hold up each picture one at a time, long enough for group members to look it over carefully. Have group members write the picture number. Then next to the number, write the immediate *feeling* or *feelings* the picture prompts. For example, a picture of a starving child in Africa might prompt feelings of pity or even disgust. (Note: It's important to stress that individuals write honest reactions and not anticipate what they *think* they should write.)

Go through the 10 pictures a second time, and have group members write next to the emotions the *action* each picture prompts. For example, the picture of the starving child might prompt action to help the child, run away or do nothing at all.

The distinction between feelings and actions is critical to this exercise. When you ask for feelings, clarify the difference between feelings and actions without revealing that you'll ask for actions later. Talk about the difference. What do your feelings and actions have in common?

☆17. *Imagine That*

Roll up a large bath towel, and secure it with string. Place the towel in the middle of the floor, and ask group members to sit around it. Ask group members each to imagine a different object the towel could represent and pick up the towel as if it were that object. If individuals have difficulty thinking of an object, here are some examples:

A live fish	A person who's fainted
A heavy suitcase	A bar of wet soap
A puppy hit by car	A stack of dishes

For another twist to this exercise, tell group members that the towel represents a baby. Ask for a volunteer to pick up the towel. Before the volunteer picks up the "baby," assign that individual a relationship *and* a circumstance from the following lists. Ask volunteers each to react according to their assignment.

Relationships	Circumstances
An inexperienced babysitter	The baby is crying
An overly strict father	The baby has a dirty diaper
An annoyed mother	The baby is sleeping
A young brother	The baby is giggling
An overly affectionate grandfather	The baby is sick
An unwed mother (or father)	The baby is screaming

As each individual completes his or her assignment, ask that person to hand the towel either to the person next to him or her or place the towel back in the center of the circle. Ask for another volunteer, and assign a new relationship and new circumstance. Make sure each group member participates.

Now that everyone has the idea, create new circumstances with the towel. See how group members handle each one. After you've used the suggestions here, be imaginative and come up with your own suggestions.

Have volunteers identify the towel as:

Item	Circumstances
● A bouquet of flowers	It's from an unwanted boyfriend or girlfriend
	It's from the casket of a loved one
	You're waiting to give it to a boyfriend or a girlfriend
● A skunk	You think it's a cat
	It's your pet
	It's injured on the road
	You're afraid of it
● An ancient scroll	You can examine in a library
	You found in a trunk in the attic
	You kept in your house because you cherish it so much; you take it out only once a year to look at it
● A case of illegal drugs	You want the drugs
	The case is handed off to you at a party—the police are at the door
	You don't know what's in the

- A box with something in it

  case or what to do with it
  You listen and hear a time bomb
  You look inside and see a snake
  You recognize it as a long-awaited package you ordered

- An unconscious body

  It's your loved one
  It's an injured person that you don't know
  It's a wounded war buddy

☆ 18. *Empathy*

We find one of Jesus' strongest commands to believers in Matthew 25:34-46. Captured within these verses is our charge to express Christ's love to all we come in contact with . . . no matter how "unlovely" they are. This exercise visually and emotionally helps demonstrate this important principle.

Ask one of your friends who's not instantly recognizable to your group members if he or she would help you illustrate an important lesson to your youth group. Have your friend dress as a derelict, wearing old, tattered clothes. You might suggest he or she use makeup or dirt to make the bumlike appearance more authentic. Prearrange a night when the derelict could visit your youth group meeting.

As the group arrives, ask the derelict to hang around in a strategic location—some place group members couldn't miss seeing him or her. Have the derelict maintain a comfortable distance, but occasionally ask different individuals what's going on inside this building. It's important that the derelict not be too forward or offensive but project a truly pathetic character.

As group members enter, make note of what they say. Who's first to notice your friend outside? Who's first to mention something to you? Who's first to suggest that something be done? Is the suggestion positive or negative? Get some casual feedback from different group members on what they think should be done.

If none of the group members suggests that you ask the derelict to join you, take the initiative. Invite the derelict in. This is particularly effective when you're having snacks prior to your meeting. Encourage group members to offer and serve the derelict something to eat.

After observing reactions, ask everyone to move chairs to the front of the room. Watch to see if any group members invite the derelict to sit next to them. Then ask one person to come forward and read Matthew 25:34-46.

As the young person reads the scripture, watch to see if anyone reacts knowingly. After the scripture reading, ask, "In light of this scripture passage, how should we react to our new friend that's visiting us?" More often than not, no one will respond. Just a few nervous bodies will shift and demonstrate a great deal of discomfort. Then ask group members, "What are your feelings at this moment?" Some brave soul may say, "Embarrassed" or "Nervous." Another individual may surprise you and say, "Sympathetic" or "Frustrated over not knowing what to do." At this point, acknowledge that all these feelings are normal and understandable. But point out that Jesus' position is clear: ". . . whatever you did for one of the least of these . . . you did for me."

At this point ask your "visitor" to come forward. Tell the group who this person really is. You'll receive varying reactions, from anger over being deceived to laughter from those who have figured out what you're doing. Whatever the case, apologize for the deception, but *don't* apologize for the lesson learned.

Use this opportunity to talk about the principle contained in these verses, and discuss what each person felt during this experience. Help group members secure those feelings in their memories. Experiences such as this not only motivate us to take action but also improve our acting skills by having specific "emotion memories" we can draw from.

★19. Concentration

One of the important keys to great acting is the ability to concentrate—to maintain one's character and lines no matter what the distractions. This simple exercise develops that ability. Ask several group members to memorize or come prepared to read a monologue from a play or famous speech such as the *Gettysburg Address*.

Emphasize the importance of developing an ability to concentrate, especially when performing. Have one of the people who have prepared ahead of time come forward as you explain what's about to happen. Ask group members to be as distractive as possible once the speech begins. Let them know they can use both verbal and visual distractions, but none can be any closer than eight feet from the speaker. Explain that audible distractions can include exuberant conversations, but no glass-shattering screams or shouts. Even though this exercise gets rowdy, it's fun to see who can maintain their composure and concentration.

☆20. *How's Your Memory?*

This simple yet fun exercise develops stronger memorization skills. Have your group members sit in a circle. Ask an individual to start the exercise by selecting a number between one and 100 and saying it aloud. Then the individual on that person's left must repeat that number and choose another number. This process continues until a person can't repeat all the numbers in the correct sequence. When a person makes an error, he or she is "out"—but just until one "memory champion" remains.

For another fun twist to this exercise, have people choose words instead of numbers. What you'll most likely find is that the words most easy to memorize have a visual image such as giraffe, bridge or airplane. Those words hardest to remember will be abstract words such as forgetful, describe or easy. This exercise not only helps improve memorization skills but also emphasizes the importance of visualizing what you're trying to memorize.

☆21. *Follow Me*

This exercise will help your group members develop their observational skills. Bring to the meeting a coat, hat, muffler, gloves and pair of snow boots. Have a volunteer come forward and put on those items. Then give him or her the following instructions: Leave the room, and when you're asked to return, walk to the front of the room and take off those five articles of clothing. While the volunteer is out of the room, instruct group members to watch every movement he or she makes and place it in their "observational memory banks."

Once the volunteer returns to the room and removes the garments, ask another volunteer to put on the clothing. After this volunteer has put on the items, instruct him or her to leave the room, return, and mimic exactly what the other individual did—from how he or she walked into the room to how and in what order each piece of clothing was removed.

Obviously, youth groups can do this same exercise in many

different ways with different items. For example, ask someone to walk in with full shopping bags and unload the items. Or walk in with a briefcase, open it and set out items to work on. Use any activity that involves a logical progression of events.

To further enhance this exercise, videotape each person and replay the tapes so people can see just how close each person was to duplicating the movements of the first individual.

☆22. *Walk This Way, Please!*

Ask different group members to walk the way they envision certain types of people to walk. Make certain that only you and the volunteer know who it is he or she is trying to emulate so that after the "walk," group members can guess what kind of person was being portrayed. Note: Be careful not to let this exercise get carried away in offensive or bigoted ways. In addition to improving observational skills, this exercise is lots of fun.

Use some of the following ideas, or create your own:

A waitress
A fashion model
A jock
A soldier marching
An astronaut on the moon
Someone wearing swimming
   fins

A hunter stalking his prey
A prisoner with shackled
   hands and feet
A person walking a dog
A hostage with a gun to his or
   her back

☆23. *Musical Mayhem*

Choose a portion of any monologue from a classical Shakespearean play such as *Hamlet* or *Macbeth*. Give volunteers a few minutes to familiarize themselves with the piece. Play different styles of music, and ask each volunteer to read the monologue to match the flavor and emotion of the music you play. Be certain that the music you select is solely instrumental so that lyrics won't confuse or alter the readers' "interpretations."

Some of the musical styles you might choose include:

Rap
Classical
Movie themes
Country

Big band
Rock
Polka
Jazz

New Age
Foreign music, such as
   Chinese or Indian

☆24. Commercial Break

This exercise works best when used as a "homework" assignment, but you also can use it on the spur of the moment. Simply have different individuals act out their favorite TV commercials in front of the group. You'll be surprised how many can remember the commercial word-for-word!

☆25. Defend Yourself

This exercise isn't for the "faint of heart." Ask a volunteer to stand in the front of the room. Tell this person that he or she is now a "defendant" in a court of law and stands accused of one of the following:

murder	not living like a Christian
theft	not trying hard enough at school
coming home after curfew	driving under the influence
(or other things you may dream up)	

Explain that the rest of the group members are the "accusers." Each accuser can ask the defendant one question that he or she must respond to. (If the group is small, allow two questions each.) Encourage the defendant to respond convincingly so that when the questioning is complete, the audience can reach a verdict of guilty or not guilty. Needless to say, the object of the exercise is for the defendant to convince the audience of his or her innocence.

☆26. Olympic Mime

Prior to this exercise, locate a videotape of some of the events in the most recent Olympic games. Show highlights of areas, such as boxing, weightlifting, swimming, skiing, bobsledding or ice skating.

After viewing these activities, assign individuals a specific sport, and have them, one at a time, pantomime the movements based on what they saw in the video or have seen live.

Sketches

Topic: *Applying biblical principles to life*

Personal Application

Preparation

Start with Warm-Up #16 (page 20) or #19 (page 24).

Sometimes we're oblivious to the way we fail to apply biblical principles to our daily activities and attitudes—yet we insist that others do so. This sketch and the discussion questions help young people recognize that attitude in themselves and talk about what they can do about it.

Characters

LIZ—the girl whose minister asks her to reach out in a service project

DOROTHY—her friend

Setting

A cafeteria or library at school before classes start

Two chairs

. . . .

(Dorothy is sitting, staring vacantly into space. Liz enters—ready for school)

LIZ   Dorothy! Sorry . . . I couldn't remember where we said we'd meet.

DOROTHY   That's all right. Have a seat.

LIZ   *(She does)* I think the idea of having morning devotions before school is a great idea—until I have to get up early to do it.

DOROTHY   I know what you mean. *(Shows her the devotional book)* I brought the book I told you about.

LIZ   Do we want to take the time this morning? I mean—it's not that long until class. Maybe we should just go straight to praying.

DOROTHY   I think we should. We agreed we wanted to read the Word.

LIZ   *(Unenthused)* Yes, I suppose we did.

DOROTHY   You don't want to?

LIZ   *(She doesn't, but hesitantly answers)* Yes . . . I do.

DOROTHY   Why don't I believe you?

LIZ   *(Pause, speaks reluctantly)* Well, Dorothy . . . I want to. I really do. But . . . my heart's not in the right frame of mind. I . . . I feel as though I need to get something cleared up.

DOROTHY   What's the matter, Liz? Is it something I've done?

LIZ   Oh, no. You're my best friend.

DOROTHY   Then what's on your mind?

LIZ   Jerry Barnes.

DOROTHY   Jerry Barnes? You mean, our youth minister Jerry Barnes?

LIZ   Yes, *that* Jerry Barnes.

DOROTHY   What's he done to get you so rattled?

LIZ   He . . . he asked me about my "walk with God." Can you believe it?

DOROTHY   Liz—that's a very *personal* question.

LIZ   It most certainly is. I mean, really . . . I hardly *know* the man.

DOROTHY Only *10* years.

LIZ Yes, I've known him 10 years . . . but I've only *known* him 10 years. He's my minister, for goodness sakes. It's not like I'm supposed to really *know* him . . . certainly not well enough for him to ask me a question like *that*.

DOROTHY I understand what you mean. *(Pause)* Well . . . how *is* your walk with God?

LIZ Why, it's . . . it's *fine*. I go to church every Sunday morning and attend the youth group meetings. He knows that. I sit almost right under his nose.

DOROTHY Then what's the problem?

LIZ He asked me to get involved in some church cleanup project or some such nonsense. I don't know what possessed him. There are other people far more . . . far more . . .

DOROTHY Suited?

LIZ Yes, *suited* for that sort of work. I said to him: "Why don't you ask Martha Dennings? She'd be *wonderful* on a project like that." He said that he'd asked her and that *she* suggested *me*. I couldn't believe it. How nervy of her.

DOROTHY Absolutely. The girl has always been nervy.

LIZ To think that *I* should be involved in a project like that. She's a troublemaker; that's what *she* is. I've never liked her. I don't know how she could go to church as often as she does and not feel overwhelmed by guilt for her attitudes.

DOROTHY I know exactly what you mean.

LIZ Of course, the whole thing made *me* look bad . . . I couldn't think of anyone else to send him to.

DOROTHY That's difficult.

LIZ Difficult isn't the word. *Impossible* . . . impossible is the word. I take my religion very seriously, and God has *yet* to reveal to me that my gift is in the area of cleaning up.

DOROTHY I've seen your room. I'll vouch for that.

LIZ And besides that—*(Pauses. Thinks about Dorothy's remark but dismisses it)* Yes. Right. So I felt very foolish about the whole experience. I wish church leaders would learn to use a little tact and diplomacy when it comes to asking us to do things.

DOROTHY Imagine them asking you to do anything at all!

LIZ I know. I know. After all the years I've sat in the services, listening to the minister preach. Surely that must count for something.

DOROTHY Surely it must.

LIZ You bet it must. *(Pauses; sighs with a sense of relief)* Well, Dorothy, I'm glad to get that off my chest. Now I feel better about studying the Bible. What are we reading?

DOROTHY Let's see . . . this little devotional book says we should read Philippians 2:1-4.

LIZ Please. Go ahead.

DOROTHY Thank you. "If you have any encouragement from being united with Christ, if any comfort from his love, if any fellowship with the Spirit, if any tenderness and compassion, then make my joy complete by being like-minded, having the same love, being one in spirit and purpose. Do nothing out of selfish ambition or vain conceit, but in humility consider others better than yourselves. Each of you should look not only to your own interests, but also to the interests of others." *(Pauses)* What beautiful words.

LIZ Yes, they are. *(Pauses)* Oh, I wish someone would show Martha Dennings those verses. She needs to hear them.

DOROTHY Maybe we could write them to her anonymously.

LIZ *(Giggles deviously)* Do you think we could?

DOROTHY Her locker's on the way to class. *(Collects her books)*

LIZ   Oh, Dorothy. Let's do it!

DOROTHY   We should.

LIZ   I mean, what good is God's Word if people won't apply it to their lives? *(They exit)*

The end.

· · · · · · · · · · · · · · · ·

Discussion Questions

1. How do you respond to people who have an attitude like Liz and Dorothy's?

2. Read James 1:22-25; John 14:15; 1 John 2:3-6; and Matthew 7:3-5. What's the problem with Liz and Dorothy's attitude? What could you say to them to help them correct their attitudes?

3. How are *you* like Liz or Dorothy in your attitudes? Explain. What can you do about it?

Topic: *Cheating*

An Opportunity

Preparation

Start with Warm-Up #3 (page 12) or #25 (page 27).

This straightforward sketch describes a young person's struggle with an opportunity to score well on a science test. Roles may be played by either gender. Close to the end, the leader will stop the action where indicated and ask the youth group to briefly discuss one question. Then the sketch will continue to its conclusion, and the group will discuss the rest of the questions.

Characters

STEVE—a concerned student who's studying for a science test

PHIL—a friend who offers Steve the answers to the test

JAN—Steve's friend from church

Setting

The school library or any other public place where one might study

A table

Two chairs

A book, paper and pencil

· · · · · · · · · · · · · · · ·

(Steve is sitting at the table, studying hard. Phil passes by, looks over his shoulder then sits down next to him)

PHIL Hey, there, Steve-o. What's going on?

STEVE Studying for that science exam. It's going to kill me. I keep going over these notes again and again, and I *still* can't get it.

PHIL This is a pretty important test for you, isn't it? I mean gradewise.

STEVE Yeah. And I didn't do so hot on the other tests either. I don't know what I'm going to do.

PHIL *(Looking around to make sure no one can hear)* I have something that'll help you.

STEVE Yeah? Like what?

PHIL Like the answers to the test.

STEVE Huh?

PHIL The answers to the test. My girlfriend got 'em when she had to stay after school last week. Mr. Bradley left them sitting on his desk, so she wrote 'em down when he was out of the room. It's all multiple choice. All you have to do is remember the sequence of the letters.

STEVE You're kidding.

PHIL Nope.

STEVE You're *sure* they're the right answers?

PHIL Absolutely.

STEVE *(Not sure what to do)* Wow!

PHIL Well?

STEVE Well, I don't know. I mean, that's . . . cheating.

PHIL You want to pass the class or not?

STEVE Yeah! But . . . it's not right, is it?

PHIL *(Shrugs)* It's not right to fail a test after you've studied hard for it either. Look, I'm just trying to give you a break.

STEVE   Yeah, I know, but . . . *(Exasperated)* I don't know. It's *cheating*.

PHIL   If you're going to keep saying that, then forget I offered.

STEVE   It is, though. Isn't it?

PHIL   It's all in how you look at it, Steve. It's not like you're cheating somebody out of something or cheating to rob somebody of their money or getting something you don't deserve. You said yourself you've studied long and hard for this test. You *deserve* to pass it!

STEVE   Yeah! I do!

PHIL   This is just a little help to insure that you will.

STEVE   Right.

PHIL   *(Takes the piece of paper out of his pocket)* Here they are.

(He extends the paper to Steve. Steve looks at it and both characters freeze)

. . . .

LEADER *Stop the sketch and ask the audience . . .*

Discussion Question

1. Should Steve take the answers? Why or why not?

. . . .

Optional Ending

(Steve reaches out and takes the paper. Phil smiles and leaves, speaking as he does)

PHIL   Smart boy. Good luck on the test.

STEVE   Thanks. *(Looks at the folded piece of paper without opening it)*

JAN   *(Enters and approaches Steve)* Hey, Steve!

STEVE   *(Guiltily tries to hide paper)* Oh . . . Hi, Jan.

JAN   I meant to tell you Sunday how much I appreciated your talk. I think you have a real gift when it comes to making the Bible practical to our everyday lives and experiences.

STEVE Gee . . . thanks.

JAN Until I heard you on Sunday, I never realized what a spiritual battle we're in—even in little things like how we act at school . . . the kinds of decisions we make. It was great.

STEVE I'm glad you got something out of it.

JAN I sure did. Well . . . see you later. *(Exits)*

STEVE *(Looks pained over the encounter. He looks at the piece of paper with an expression of helplessness then looks at the audience and exits without unfolding the paper)*

The end.

. . . .

Discussion Questions (continued)

2. Have you ever been in a situation like this? How did you feel? What was the outcome? What did you learn from the experience?

3. What is the biblical attitude toward cheating? Read Genesis 27:1-45. Can you think of other biblical characters who cheated? What were the consequences? Is there ever a good reason for cheating?

4. "Cheating is wrong only if you get caught." Do you agree or disagree? Why?

Consider Phil's attitude: "Cheating is wrong only if you're taking something that isn't yours, but it's all right if you think you deserve something." Do you agree or disagree? Why?

Body-Building

Preparation

Start with Warm-Up #8 (page 15), #13 (page 19) or #26 (page 27).

Here's a sketch to go crazy with. You may want to make a sign for each character, or group members can have fun designing costumes for their characters. Be as outrageous as your group's tastes allow. Encourage participants to enjoy themselves and milk the bad jokes as much as possible.

Before you begin this sketch, ask a young person to read 1 Corinthians 12. The message of church involvement will make itself clear.

Characters

BRAIN—stereotypically intelligent manner and appearance
CELL—functional appearance, an assistant to Brain
LIMBS—muscular and tough
MOUTH—loud manner and appearance
HEART—unassuming and gentle; sensitive

Setting

Five chairs in a semicircle facing the audience; should look like a meeting

· · · · · · · · · · · · · · ·

Note

(All enter, talking among themselves. Characters each carry a pad of paper and a pencil or pen as if they're attending a business meeting. They should seat themselves in this order from left to right: Heart, Mouth, Cell, Brain and Limbs)

BRAIN   *(Trying to establish order)* Okay, gang, let's get started. *(Looks around)* Are these all the delegates? *(To Cell)* Cell, please check the roll.

CELL   Sure, Brain. *(Reading off a list)* Brain and related functions.

BRAIN   That's me, I think.

CELL   Limbs—representative for arms, legs, feet, hands, and subdivisions of fingers and toes.

LIMBS   Yo!

CELL   Mouth.

MOUTH   *(Loudly)* Here!

BRAIN   Where's Tongue?

MOUTH   Couldn't make it. The Landlord had a peanut butter sandwich a little while ago, and he's somewhat hung up—if you know what I mean.

CELL   Eyes and Ears.

(No answer)

CELL   Eyes and Ears?

MOUTH   Oh, me again. I'm sorry. They asked me to speak for them.

CELL   Heart and internal organs.

HEART   That's me. And let me say that I'm very happy to be here.

LIMBS   Can we get going? These meetings always make me stiff.

BRAIN   Fine. I thought we should get together because . . . well, frankly, I think we have a problem.

ALL   *(Respond with comments such as "A problem? What kind of problem?")*

BRAIN As you know, we all try very hard to work well together.

LIMBS *(Obviously directed to Mouth) Some* of us do.

MOUTH What's that supposed to mean?

LIMBS You know exactly what it means.

MOUTH I don't *know* anything—I'm just a Mouth. *(To Brain)* What *does* he mean?

BRAIN The *toe* incident.

MOUTH The *toe* incident! Give me a break.

LIMBS I'd like to.

HEART No! That would hurt all of us.

MOUTH Look, Limbs, I . . .

LIMBS Looking is *your* department.

MOUTH You know what I mean.

LIMBS I don't *know* anything either. I'm just in charge of limbs. I can "strong-arm," I can "get a leg up," I can "put my foot down," I can "lend a hand," I can "make elbow-room," but I can't *know* anything.

BRAIN An expression of speech, Limbs. Please cooperate.

MOUTH *You're* the one who rammed those toes into the wall.

LIMBS That's because *your* department wasn't watching where you were going.

MOUTH Wrong! Brain has it fully documented by Memory that we tried to tell you.

BRAIN That's true. I sent a memo your way immediately.

MOUTH And you *still* hit the wall.

LIMBS Look, by the time we got the message it was too late to stop. Hey, we're only human!

MOUTH And what are we—chopped liver?

HEART Watch it.

MOUTH Sorry. I mention it only because Tongue still hasn't recovered from the verbal abuse he had to say. And I'm still a little shaken myself . . . all those bad words . . .

BRAIN   That was my fault. An automatic response. Eyes have been reading too many popular novels. If I get filled with too much of that stuff, it becomes difficult to control my output.

MOUTH   Oh, great! Eyes gets the blame again. Why is everyone always picking on Eyes? You know, they have half a mind to stage a walkout.

LIMBS   That I'd like to see.

MOUTH   You *can't*. Ha! Ha!

BRAIN   I don't think it's physically possible for Eyes to walk out either. But it *is* possible for us to put a foot in our mouths.

LIMBS   I can arrange that.

MOUTH   Oh . . . aren't we the macho one today!

LIMBS   If you'd stop shooting yourself off . . .

HEART   Please! Please! I suggest we stop this fighting. It hurts me when we argue. I really take a beating.

BRAIN   Heart's right.

HEART   To the left, actually.

BRAIN   Let's get on with this. We have serious matters to discuss.

LIMBS   *What* serious matters? I don't get it. I've never been in better shape.

BRAIN   In a way, that's the problem. Our Landlord has been giving you a great workout while the rest of us remain idle. All indications are that this isn't healthy for the entire body.

LIMBS   Health! Who cares about health? I just need to look better than the rest of you.

BRAIN   I think Face would argue with that.

LIMBS   By the way, where *is* Face?

BRAIN   He had a bit of trouble with acne. He's trying to save himself.

HEART   Vanity. It's all vanity. How one looks is hardly representative of one's importance here.

LIMBS   Tell that to the Landlord.

HEART   I've tried.

BRAIN   Here's the situation: Eyes reported to me about a book they saw recently.

CELL   The Bible.

BRAIN   Thank you. The Bible.

LIMBS   I know about that book. We're always moving it out of the way.

BRAIN   The Landlord read a part of it recently that discussed building up the entire body as opposed to just parts of it. I think it's a valid idea.

MOUTH   Of course it is! It's a wonderful idea.

LIMBS   What are you yapping about? You get a bigger workout than anyone!

MOUTH   I was just agreeing. Will you leave me alone?

HEART   Yes, Limbs—you need to get off Mouth's back.

LIMBS   I'm sorry. It's just my "tendon-cy."

BRAIN   All right, all right. We'll make up later. The point is this: I want to give the Landlord an idea of a total fitness program—a general health program—a complete body buildup, if you will. Heart'll back me up—won't you?

HEART   Poor choice of words.

BRAIN   You'll support the idea?

HEART   Of course. I'm for anything that'll benefit the entire body.

LIMBS   What a guy. You're all heart.

HEART   In a manner of speaking.

BRAIN   Are we agreed then? All in favor, say "Aye."

ALL   Aye.

BRAIN   The ayes have it.

MOUTH   They'll be happy to hear that.

BRAIN   If that's it, we can adjourn. I'll call a meeting of the Ideas and Suggestions department along with Discipline and Willpower. I'll give you their responses at the next meeting.

LIMBS   I bet we'll find out without you telling us.

BRAIN   Let me close by saying that this could be the most important endeavor we've all been involved in. Our unity is necessary for this to work as it should. Agreed? *(All nod yes)* Great. Let's go.

(They move in unison toward the exit. As they do, Limbs speaks to Brain)

LIMBS   I gotta hand it to you, Brain. You've really got a head on your shoulders. *(All characters exit)*

The end.

. . . .

Discussion Questions

1. Beyond the comedy, what is this sketch about?

2. Read 1 Corinthians 12 again. What does this scripture passage tell you about the church and how it operates like a body? Do you know what your place in the body is? If you do, explain what it is and why you think so. If you don't know, how can you find your place in the body?

3. What does your membership in the body mean in terms of:
  ● church attendance?
  ● involvement?
  ● commitment?
  ● compassion?
  ● friendships?

Listening

Preparation

Start with Warm-Up #13 (page 19) or #19 (page 24).

This sketch examines a conversation in which both people are talking, but neither are listening. For an interesting approach, after the sketch is presented, have characters read their lines again simultaneously.

Characters

JACKIE

RAY

Setting

A bench, or a couple of chairs

. . . .

(Jackie and Ray sit on a bench)

JACKIE You're looking kinda down. Something wrong?

RAY Nah.

JACKIE Come on . . . what is it?

RAY It's . . . well, it's my parents. You know.

Note

JACKIE	Yeah, I know. My dad and I got into it last night.
RAY	Me too. He said I wasn't spending enough time on my homework.
JACKIE	Mine said I wasn't helping around the house enough.
RAY	It wouldn't be so bad if he didn't yell at me. Maybe I'd agree if he didn't yell.
JACKIE	He said my room is always a mess. I don't think my room is messy. Do you think my room's a mess?
RAY	He gets all red in the face and says things that I *hope* he doesn't mean. I mean, he can be so . . . cruel. Mom just stands there.
JACKIE	I pick things up . . . usually. Once I left some of my clothes in the bathroom, and I thought he was going to throw me out of the house. He's such a perfectionist. Nothing ever satisfies him.
RAY	He's obsessed with my grades. I have to make good grades . . . nothing less than an A. *(Chuckles sadly)* What's sad is that I don't think it has anything to do with his wanting me to do good. I guess he does. But . . . well . . .
JACKIE	He folds all his clothes neatly. Everything in his closet is hung just right. He also cleans out his wallet once a week. *(Laughs)* He even drives Mom nuts sometimes.
RAY	I think he's more concerned with how my grades make *him* look. Know what I mean? He wants his kid to make good grades so everyone'll be impressed with what a good father he is.
JACKIE	One day I'm going to trash his bedroom. Y' know? I'm gonna run in and throw his clothes all over the place—just to see what he does.
RAY	*(Sighs)* I guess I'll try to spend more time on my homework . . . if it'll keep him off my back. I get so tired of fighting about it.

(A moment of silence)

RAY	Guess I'd better get going. Thanks for listening, Jackie. It's nice to have someone to talk to.

JACKIE Yeah. Glad I could help. *(Both exit)*

The end.

. . . .

Discussion Questions

1. When have you had a conversation like this? Who was it with? What was the outcome? How did you feel? How do you think the other person felt?

2. Are you a good listener? Why or why not? Think of someone you believe is a good listener. What does that person do that qualifies him or her as a good listener? Is "good listening" merely sitting there while someone else talks? Why or why not?

3. Regardless of whether you think you're a good listener or not, how can you become a *better* listener?

4. Who would you classify as a good listener—your parents? your teachers? your youth worker at church? your minister? For each person you identify, explain why he or she is a good listener. How could he or she improve? How can you improve your communication to help that person become a better listener? How can *you* be a better listener to each of these individuals?

5. What prevents us from being good listeners?

6. Read Proverbs 18:13 and James 1:19.

7. Do our listening and communication habits affect how we listen to and communicate with God? Explain.

Topic: *Consequences*

The Accident

Preparation

Start with Warm-Up #3 (page 12) or #4 (page 13).

The basic idea behind this sketch is to demonstrate a young man's reaction to wrecking his dad's car—especially when he takes the car against his parent's wishes. This sketch will help young people talk about how to accept the consequences of their actions.

Characters

JOSH—a teenager who has wrecked his dad's car

LYNN—Josh's teenage girlfriend who was with him in the accident

FATHER—*(Voice only)*

Setting

Josh's living room

A couch and a chair (Use folding chairs if you wish)

Anything else you want to add for the sake of the environment

. . . .

(Josh and Lynn enter. Lynn looks a bit frazzled, while Josh is downright frantic. During the "Oh goshes" he paces the floor and wrings his hands or puts his hands in and out of his pants pockets)

JOSH   Oh gosh, oh gosh, oh gosh, ohgoshohgoshohgosh! What am I gonna do? It's wrecked. It's wrecked. *The car . . . is . . . wrecked!*

LYNN   We almost died. My life's still passing in front of my eyes. I didn't know so much has happened to me in 16 years.

JOSH   I won't make it to 17. Dad's gonna kill me. Oh gosh, oh gosh. Ohgoshohgoshohgosh! Who put it there? That's what I want to know. Who *put it there*?

LYNN   What?

JOSH   The fire hydrant. Who put it there? That corner is the worst corner in the universe to put a fire hydrant on! I'm going to write my congressman. That's what I'll do. I'll write and tell him how incredibly stupid it was to put a fire hydrant there.

LYNN   But it's always been there.

JOSH   Not anymore. Now it's a hood ornament! Oh gosh! Oh gosh! The car's wrecked. It's totaled. What am I going to tell my dad? What am I supposed to say? My life's over.

LYNN   Tell him the truth—

JOSH   The truth! Are you *crazy*? Some girlfriend you are! This is my dad's car I'm talking about! I can't tell him the truth!

LYNN   What else can you tell him? That the fire hydrant ran down the street and attacked your car in the driveway?

JOSH   I don't know. I don't know. I've got to pack. I'll go to Mexico or Canada. Oh gosh! Oh gosh! Ohgoshohgosh-ohgosh!

LYNN   Will you please stop with the "Oh goshes"?

JOSH   I can't. It helps me think. What am I going to say to my dad? What'll I tell my parents? They'll be home soon!

LYNN   The truth, Josh.

JOSH   But you don't understand! *I wasn't supposed to take the* *car!* The last thing they said to me before they left was not to drive the car because it needed work on the steering.

Oh gosh. Oh gosh. They're going to lock me in the closet and push bread crumbs under the door for the rest of my life. Help me, will you? I need a good story!

LYNN   Tell them the truth, Josh. Your parents are great. They'll understand.

JOSH   How could they understand? *I* wouldn't understand! If my kid had done this, I'd have him put to sleep. This is beyond understanding, Lynn. This is *my dad's car.*

LYNN   Josh, I'm sure they love you more than that car. In fact, once they see the car, they'll consider it a miracle that you're alive!

JOSH   Don't count on it. Don't count on it. Once they see the car, they'll consider it an *act of God* that I lived just so they can have the pleasure of punishing me.

LYNN   You're exaggerating.

JOSH   Why did I do it, Lynn? *Why did I do it?* They told me not to take the car, and I did it anyway! What brain cells died at my birth to let me do such a stupid thing?

I know—it's genetic. Generations of stupidity. Original sin—that's what it is. We learned about it last week in Sunday school. *(Laughs without meaning to)* That's it—it's not my fault! It's Adam and Eve—*they* blew it!

LYNN   Josh, why don't you sit down?

JOSH   Oh gosh. Oh gosh . . .

LYNN   Here we go again. *(Mimics Josh as they pace back and forth)*

JOSH   Ohgoshohgoshohgosh! They said, "Don't take the car." Just like God said, "Don't bite the apple." If they hadn't told me *not* to take the car, then . . .

LYNN   You'd have taken it anyway. I think you must have hit your head on something.

JOSH   I did . . . against the wall of my future—short, dark and bleak. Oh, Lynn, . . . *(Drops onto couch)* what am I going to say? I have to make up something really believable. *(Jumps to his feet again, pacing)*

LYNN   Tell them what really happened, Josh. Maybe you'll get punished, but at least you'll have told the truth.

JOSH   I don't want to get punished.

LYNN   Maybe they won't punish you because you were honorable enough to tell the truth.

JOSH   *(Stops completely; looks at Lynn)* You don't really believe that, do you?

LYNN   No.

JOSH   Good. For a minute there I thought *you* might have a concussion. *(Paces again)* Would the weather be better in Canada or Mexico?

LYNN   Josh, now *stop it*! Listen to me. *(Gets his attention)* Don't you see what this is? This is your moment—your own personal fork in the road. It's the time when all your years of Sunday school and upbringing stand against the test of this crisis. Your morality is on the line! Your parents are going to walk through that door, and you're going to decide whether to tell them the truth or lie your way out of it. Don't you see?

JOSH   Really? *(Taken aback by this kind of thinking, he pauses to consider it)* You're right, Lynn. You're right. This is it, isn't it? My moment. My own personal crisis. My morality. *(Stands still and takes a deep breath as if to agree)*

LYNN   Good for you, Josh. I knew I wasn't dating a slouch.

(Offstage we hear the front door slam and the sound of Josh's father shouting angrily . . .)

FATHER Joshua Robert!

JOSH   *(Looks at Lynn with great determination; takes two steps toward voice; suddenly grabs Lynn's hand and pulls her the opposite direction)* Mexico has better food! *(They run off)*

The end.

. . . .

Discussion Questions

1. Discuss Josh's character. Was he right or wrong in taking the car? wrecking the car? avoiding his parents? Be honest. What would you have done if you were in Josh's position? Has anyone in this group had a similar situation? Describe what happened.

2. Is "honesty always the best policy"—even if the consequences will be painful? Why or why not? Think of a situation when you did something wrong and had to suffer for it. What did you learn?

What are the merits, if any, of avoiding the consequences of wrong actions? In other words, if you can get out of a wrongdoing without suffering for it, should you? Why or why not?

3. Read the story of David and Bathsheba (2 Samuel 11—12:1-25). What were David's actions and their consequences? Even though God forgave David for his sins, certain consequences still took place—then and for the rest of David's life. What conclusions might you draw from this story?

Topic: *Dating Attitudes*

The Kiss

Preparation

Start with Warm-Up #11 (page 18) or #22 (page 26).

Many teenagers feel that money spent during a night out with someone of the opposite sex is sort of a "down payment" for what's to happen at the end of the evening. This sketch helps kids discuss their dating expectations. It also offers them an opportunity to see how their Christian values play a part in dating.

Ask characters to deliver their lines briskly and energetically.

Characters

KEN—the guy with a date
CRAIG—Ken's brother
FATHER—Ken and Craig's father

Setting

A living room
Two chairs

(Ken and Craig enter talking)

KEN   Do you know what I'm telling you? Do you *know* what

I'm telling you?

CRAIG   No. What are you telling me? I asked you where you went last night. I got home from practice and you were gone.

KEN   I'm telling you Barbara—that's what I'm telling you.

CRAIG   Barbara?

KEN   Isn't that what I said? Is that *not* what I said?

CRAIG   You said Barbara.

KEN   I said Barbara and *me*—that's what I said. Are you listening to me?

CRAIG   I'm listening. You . . .

KEN   And Barbara.

CRAIG   Barbara.

KEN   Barbara.

CRAIG   *You* and Barbara?

KEN   What's my name? Me and Barbara on a *date*.

CRAIG   You're kidding. A date? Tell me you're kidding.

KEN   I'm telling you—me and Barbara on a by-ourselves-completely-alone-dream-come-true-kinda-date. How can I tell you?

CRAIG   In detail.

KEN   You want details? Unbelievable. How's that for detail? *Unbelievable*.

CRAIG   You kissed her?

KEN   Kissed her. Did I hear you right? *Kissed* her? Do you know what I'm telling you? Do you have *any idea* what I'm telling you?

CRAIG   She's a good kisser?

KEN   What did I say? Didn't I say unbelievable?

CRAIG   That's what you said.

KEN   I won't say it again.

CRAIG   You don't have to. So where were you? on the front
        porch? in the car? Where?

KEN   Where? What is where? This is Barbara I'm talking
        about. This is me and Barbara and candlelight at
        Monique's.

CRAIG   You took her to *Monique's*? They have cloth napkins.
        You can't afford Monique's.

KEN   Monique's.

CRAIG   Is that where you kissed her?

KEN   Get out of the Lookout Point mentality, will you? I'm
        talking Barbara. I'm talking me. I'm talking Monique's.
        I'm talking a play.

CRAIG   Who played?

KEN   Actors, actresses, the *stage*.

CRAIG   You kissed her at a play?

KEN   Am I the kind of person to kiss at a play?

CRAIG   You'd kiss anywhere you could get away with it.

KEN   You're a pervert.

CRAIG   I'm your brother.

KEN   Are you going to shut up and listen, or maybe I'll keep
        it to myself?

CRAIG   I'll shut up.

KEN   And listen?

CRAIG   I'm listening.

*(At this point their father enters silently behind them. Unnoticed,
he stops to listen)*

KEN   Good 'cause when we get back to her house—and I
        mean *house*. I mean *mansion* is what I mean—she in-
        vites me in—yes, *invites* me is what I said. The place is
        quiet. Everyone's in bed. We sit down on the couch,
        and what am I thinking?

CRAIG   You're thinking about her lips.

KEN   I'm thinking that this is Barbara and me, that's what I'm thinking.

CRAIG   And that's when you kissed her.

KEN   I'm *thinking*, that's what I'm saying. And she smiles at me as only Barbara can smile.

CRAIG   I know that smile.

KEN   And she thanks me for a wonderful night out and—can you believe it?—she thanks me for being a perfect gentleman. What's my name? I said *gentleman*.

CRAIG   And that's when you kissed her.

KEN   A *gentleman* she said—and I'm looking into those eyes. Those *Barbara* eyes.

CRAIG   I know those eyes.

KEN   She kissed me.

CRAIG   *(In disbelief) What*?!?

KEN   Right here on the cheek.

CRAIG   Oh man, oh man—*(Excited, he stops; then pauses briefly)* the *cheek*!

KEN   Boom. Right there.

CRAIG   And that's when you kissed her.

KEN   Nope. That was it. It was unbelievable. A perfect gentleman.

CRAIG   The cheek. All that for a kiss on the cheek.

KEN   Yep.

CRAIG   But Monique's, the play . . . a kiss on the *cheek*?

KEN   Are you listening to me? You're not listening to me. I'm telling you something here. We've got it all wrong. It's not the money. It's not an investment for an end-of-the-night payoff. Respect is what I'm telling you. It's the person you're with. It was the best kiss I ever had.

FATHER   *(Speaks, startling them)* Boys, it's time for dinner.

CRAIG   *(Speaking to Ken)* You're out of your mind. *(Gets up to*

> *exit past Father)* You've flipped your gourd. *(To Father)*
> Call the boys from the Rubber Room, Dad; he's lost it.
> *(Exits)*

(Ken moves to exit past Father as well, but Father stops him)

FATHER   Ken, I know I don't say it much—but sometimes I'm really proud of how you're turning out.

KEN   You know what, Dad? *(Pause)* So am I. *(They exit to go eat)*

The end.

· · · · · · · · · · · · · · · · ·

Discussion Questions

1. For the guys: When you go out on a first date with a girl, do you have any expectation about getting a kiss good night? If you don't, why not? If you do, what do you base your expectation on? (For example: the girl? her reputation? what you do that night? how much you spend?)

On subsequent dates with a girl, what are your expectations for a kiss good night and why?

2. For the girls: On a first date with a guy, what is your expectation about kissing at the end of the evening? Do you feel any pressure about kissing? If you don't, why not? If you do, what causes this pressure? (For example: something he says? something he does? how much money he's spent on you? fear of what he might think? fear of what others might think?)

On subsequent dates, do you feel obligated to kiss good night? Why or why not?

3. What's the purpose of a good night kiss? Explain.

4. How would you define "being a gentleman" on a date? a "lady"?

5. What would be the "Christian" view, if any, to all of these questions? What does the Bible say about dating and dating behavior? (See Philippians 4:8 for a start on this discussion.)

Too Far

Preparation

Start with Warm-Up #6 (page 14) or #8 (page 15).

This sketch deals with a controversial yet common question: "How far should I go?" Rather than provide answers, the sketch offers two endings. As the leader, help your group choose one or the other. Or just for kicks, play out both endings, and ask the audience which would be right. This sketch should stimulate discussion, and the questions should help your group members find some answers.

Characters

DONNA—the girlfriend
CARL—the boyfriend

Setting

Donna's living room; can be as simple or as elaborate as you like

. . . .

(Donna enters and sits down angrily. Carl follows. They've just returned from a date)

CARL   *(Apologetically)* Donna . . . Look, I said I'm sorry.

DONNA   Keep your voice down. I don't want to wake up my folks.

CARL   What do you want me to do—huh? I'm sorry. I don't know what happened.

DONNA   I do.

CARL   Yeah, well, I mean, I *know* what happened, but I don't know *why* it happened. I mean . . . I lost control.

DONNA   We shouldn't have gone to Lookout Point. People go to Lookout Point for *one* thing.

CARL   Not true. I didn't take you up there for that reason.

DONNA   *(Not believing him)* No?

CARL   No! I just wanted to be alone with you . . . to talk.

DONNA   What *kind* of talk—*body* language?

CARL   That's not fair.

DONNA   How can I be fair? I asked you to stop and you didn't. I nearly had to scream, and what did you do? You got mad at me.

CARL   I got . . . frustrated.

DONNA   I understand that—but, good grief, Carl . . . what kind of girl do you think I am? *(Pause)* No—I think you answered that question tonight.

CARL   I didn't! It's not like that! I like you a lot, Donna. Maybe more than any other girl I've ever liked before. And . . . well, I got carried away. Something switched off and . . . I lost control. It'll never happen again. I swear.

DONNA   Why should I believe you?

CARL   Because it *won't*—that's why. I respect you too much to let it happen again. Give me another chance, will you?

DONNA   Another chance to do *what*? It's always the same thing, isn't it? First a little kissing and then a lot of kissing and then hands all over the place. It's like going out with an octopus. I don't know if I can trust you again . . . to give you another chance.

CARL   You can . . . I mean it. I'll take ice baths before I'll let it happen again. *(Pause)* Please? I'm sorry. Just tell me what you want me to do.

DONNA I want you to go home—now.

CARL But, Donna . . .

DONNA Really, Carl. I want you to leave.

(They stand looking at each other a moment)

DONNA Now.

CARL All right, all right. Can I call you tomorrow?

(Both characters should freeze in position)

· · · · · · · · · · · · · · · ·

(LEADER: Ask the group, "Should she say yes or no?" Based on the group's response, have the characters perform one of the following endings)

Optional ending if she says yes:

DONNA *(Long pause)* Yeah, I guess. But I mean it: if this ever happens again, it's over. I don't know what happened between you and other girls, but I don't think it's right.

CARL Right. It won't. You can trust me. *(Pause)* Can I have a kiss good night?

DONNA Go home, Carl.

CARL Yeah. Right. *(Exits)*

The end.

· · · · · · · · · · · · · · · ·

Optional ending if she says no:

DONNA *(Long pause)* No, Carl. I . . . I don't think that's a good idea. Let's take some time off . . . from each other to . . . think about this.

CARL But . . . *(Pause)* I don't know why it has to be such a big deal.

DONNA Good night, Carl.

CARL   Yeah. Good night. *(Exits)*

The end.

. . . .

Discussion Questions

1. What do you think Carl tried to do? Assuming he tried to have sex with Donna, was she right for stopping him when she did? Why or why not?

2. What are a girl's reasons for saying no to sex? Beyond a fear of pregnancy, AIDS or venereal diseases, why else should a girl say no? What, if any, are good reasons for a girl to say yes?

3. Was Carl right or wrong in his attitude during the date? after the date? He promised that it would never happen again. Did you believe him? Why or why not?

4. Why does it seem that the burden of saying no usually falls to the girl?

5. "I'm a Christian, and I think my boyfriend (or girlfriend) and I can do whatever we want as long as we don't actually have sex." Is this statement right or wrong? Why?

6. Read the following Bible verses. Give a practical application for each one.

    1 Corinthians 6:18-20
    2 Corinthians 6:14-18
    Galatians 5:13, 16-24
    Philippians 4:8
    2 Timothy 2:22
    Titus 2:7-8

According to these passages, is there an acceptable time to say yes? Does the Bible say anything about a sexual relationship outside of marriage?

7. In what practical ways can this situation—and situations like it—be avoided? (A hint: Lookout Point.)

Topic: *Death*

Brad and His Friends

Preparation

Start with Warm-Up #6 (page 14) or #8 (page 15). Use Warm-Up #5 (page 13) in the Discussion Questions.

Three young people react to a tragic car accident that killed a group of their friends. Characters can be either gender and should *not* appear as if they're engaged in a conversation—even though they're on stage together. (Create the feeling of an interview in which the camera moves from one person to another.)

Characters

FRIEND 1
FRIEND 2
FRIEND 3

Setting

A plain stage
Characters can either sit on stools or stand

. . . .

(Three people enter and take their places on stage. Characters should ignore each other and speak directly to the audience)

FRIEND 1 I heard a rumor that they're going to bring in a special counselor at school. The guy's supposed to be some kinda expert. He's going to talk to us. I don't know what he thinks he's going to say.

Pretty dumb idea, if you ask me. I mean, what can *anybody* say? They're dead. Talking about it won't bring them back. I mean, yeah, I'm sorry they're gone. I miss 'em. But I wish everyone would stop making such a big deal about it. You know?

(PAUSE)

FRIEND 2 Last night I had a dream about Brad. We were standing in the school parking lot talking—right before they left. *Right* before. Just like it was that day.

Friends say I was the last person to talk to them. They wanted to know what we'd talked about. Paper clips. Brad was saying how he hated chemistry class and made paper clips into little animals to keep from bein' bored. That's what we talked about. It got pretty rude, really.

Then they left—the four of them. I watched them pull out. Johnny blew kisses at me through the back window. Johnny was always a little weird.

FRIEND 3 *Was.* I can't believe I have to talk about them in the past tense.

FRIEND 2 In my dream, I took Brad's car keys away from him and threw them down the sewer. He got really mad . . . but he didn't die. None of them did. I know it's stupid, but you wanna know what's *really* dumb? I woke up crying.

(PAUSE)

FRIEND 1 I didn't go to the funeral. We had one of our own. A bunch of us went out and got blitzed. It was great. I drove home and almost hit a tree. It was funny. I mean, we wondered what everyone would do if we got killed—you know, right after Brad and those guys.

They'd probably bring in *two* special counselors. Ha.

FRIEND 3 I heard that the truck that hit them went through the light without even *trying* to stop. They probably didn't even know what happened.

(PAUSE)

FRIEND 2 I was thinking about how we talked about paper clips. I thought if we *hadn't* taken the time to talk, Brad would've been through the intersection *before* the truck. Or if we talked longer, the truck would've already gone through. Man, it messes up my mind. One minute either way would've saved their lives.

FRIEND 3 All the adults keep talking about what a waste it is. They say Brad and Johnny and Steve and Bob had so much potential. They say the *future* lost four great people. But what about *us*?

FRIEND 2 I never thought about the future. Not really. Until *this* happened. Now . . . now I wonder about it. I don't wanna be creepy or morbid, but I keep thinking about death. *My* death.

FRIEND 1 I guess if I have to die, that's the best way to go. Quick. No thinking about it. No pain. My grandma died of cancer, and it was terrible. It took *so long*.

FRIEND 3 It's one thing when *old people* die. I guess I always figured they were supposed to. But Brad and Johnny— those guys were *my* age.

FRIEND 1 It happens, you know? That's the way it is. Nothing you can do when your number's up. Just have a good time until it happens.

(PAUSE)

FRIEND 2 *(Thoughtfully)* I wonder if there's a way to . . . to get ready to die. Know what I mean? How do you *prepare* for it? What would Brad have done if somehow he knew he was going to die at that moment? I think of all the "What ifs" and wonder, "What would I do different?" and all that. But *how can I know*? How can anyone know? Suddenly, it's over. *(Pause)* Poor Brad.

FRIEND 3 Poor *us. (They exit)*

The end.

· · · · · · · · · · · · · · · · ·

Discussion Questions

1. Imagine you've just lost a group of your friends in a car wreck. How would *you* react? Which person in the sketch do you relate to most? Why?

2. Do you ever think about death? If not, why not? If so, what do you think about death?

(NOTE: After this question, do Warm-Up #5.)

3. Can a person prepare for death? If so, how?

4. What does the Bible say about death? What is a "proper Christian attitude" about death (if such a thing exists)? Read John 11:25-26; 14:1-4; Romans 8:35-39; and 2 Corinthians 5:1. What do these scripture passages mean to you?

5. Write your obituary. Include how and at what age you died. How do you want others to remember you—for what you did or for who you were? Is there a difference? Why or why not?

Farewell

Preparation

Start with Warm-Up #15 (page 20) or #21 (page 25).

This sketch emphasizes the importance of family memories—regardless of where we are. During a family move, a brother and sister stand in an empty room and reminisce about their experiences there. Their conversation demonstrates that goodbyes are hard when so much is attached to what we say goodbye to.

Characters

KEITH

DEBORAH

Setting

An empty family room

(Keith enters, ponders the room silently and sighs because of its barrenness. Deborah enters)

DEBORAH   Keith, Dad says to hurry up. He wants to get to the hotel before dark.

KEITH   Okay.

(Keith doesn't move. Deborah starts to leave but notices that her brother isn't following)

DEBORAH   Keith? I think he meant *now*.

KEITH   I know. I just wanted a last look. That's all.

DEBORAH   You're not getting all sentimental, are you?

KEITH   Of course not. *(Pause)* Well, maybe a little. Don't you feel . . . sad?

DEBORAH   Don't be silly. I was doing my Niagara Falls imitation at the going-away party last night. Didn't you notice?

KEITH   I thought that was because Eddie didn't kiss you goodbye.

DEBORAH   You're a jerk.

KEITH   I don't know what you like about him.

DEBORAH   I guess it doesn't make much difference now, does it?

KEITH   I guess not. *(Sadly)* None of it does.

DEBORAH   Cut it out, Keith. You're so . . . *bleak*. You have to think of this as a . . . as a new adventure. A new school, new friends . . . it's a new challenge for you. A new chapter. A new beginning. A new . . .

KEITH   Did Mom and Dad pay you to say this, or are you just practicing for your own kids?

DEBORAH   Go ahead. Sulk if you want to, but hurry up. They're waiting in the car. *(She moves to exit but stops when he speaks)*

KEITH   We did most of our growing up in here, Deborah. Everything I can remember relates to this room. *(Pause)* I don't know why Dad had to take that job.

DEBORAH   Sure you do.

KEITH   I *know* I do . . . but I don't really. *So* it's a good career move, *so* he'll be making more money, *so* it's where he believes God wants him. Give me *good* reasons. He's taking me away from the house I grew up in.

DEBORAH   You're really serious about this, aren't you?

KEITH   Yes . . . I am. Don't you feel it? I mean, you have as many memories as I do. This is where it happened—*(Pause, looking around, he speaks softly)*—all the Christmas trees and presents.

DEBORAH   *(Remembering, smiling)* You used to be in charge of decorating in here. Whatever happened to that cardboard chimney you used to put all our stockings on?

KEITH   It was the first thing Dad burned when we got a *real* chimney. *(Pause)* Do you remember that surprise birthday party you guys gave me?

DEBORAH   Yeah. Mom took you shopping to get you out of the house, and you moped the whole time.

KEITH   But I was really surprised when we got home. See? It was all in here . . . the games I played with you and Mom and Dad. Remember? Dad taught me to play chess in here.

DEBORAH   This is where we had our slumber parties too . . .

KEITH   We played hide-and-seek, Monopoly, and . . . oh, I remember the night I played spin the bottle with Karen and Andrea . . .

DEBORAH   *(Pointing)* I had all my dolls set up in *that* corner . . .

KEITH   Remember when we covered the walls with those superhero posters? There wasn't an inch of paneling left.

DEBORAH   This is weird, Keith. I've never seen you like this before. You're actually being . . . *human*.

KEITH   What am I usually?

DEBORAH   Please. You're depressed enough.

KEITH   This is *home*, Deb. We're leaving our home.

DEBORAH   *(She looks around at the emptiness for a moment)* What—this? Nah. Now it's just a house. *(Exits)* Come on . . .

KEITH   *(Lingers, considering her comment)* Yeah . . . I guess you're right. It *is* just a house. *(Exits)*

The end.

. . . .

Discussion Questions

1. What's the difference between a "house" and a "home"? Which do you live in—a house or a home? Explain. Read Psalm 127 and Matthew 7:24-27. How do these scripture passages apply, or do they? Explain your answer.

2. What good things do you remember about when you were younger? What bad things? What kind of relationship did you have with your parents? your brothers or sisters? How have those relationships changed?

3. In the house where you grew up, is there a particular room that triggers more memories (good or bad) than other rooms? Which room was it, and what do you remember?

4. Think of one activity your family did together when you were younger. What was it? Does your family still do it together? What kinds of family activities do you now do? What kinds of activities do you *wish* your family would do together?

5. List activities you could do with your family. Circle the activities you would actually suggest. How do you think your family members would react?

6. If you've moved from the house where you were raised, how did you feel when you moved? What do you miss most about the house? If you could change the place you live now, how would you change it?

7. If you still live in the house where you grew up, think about how you would feel if you had to move. What would you miss most? What hopes would you have for the house you'd move into?

Topic: *Family quirks*

The Punishment

Preparation

Start with Warm-Up #2 (page 12), #13 (page 19) or #14 (page 20).

Have you ever felt your parents weren't speaking the same language as you? Have you ever felt they said one thing, but their attitudes revealed another? This sketch demonstrates how a young person feels about his actions and the punishment he received.

A talented group member can perform this sketch as a monologue. Or characters can perform in an imaginary setting as David delivers the monologue.

Characters

DAVID

MOTHER

FATHER

Setting

A family room

Chair

An imaginary bedroom

. . . .

(David enters. His demeanor suits the occasion—he's being punished. His mother follows and points to the couch)

MOTHER   You plant it right there, Buster Brown, until you've learned your lesson. I just want you to sit there and *think. (Exits)*

(David sits down, stands, moves to the television and reaches to turn it on)

MOTHER   *(From offstage)* No TV either!

DAVID   *(Withdraws his hand and sits down on the couch. He looks miserable. Then after a few moments of painful silence, he speaks to the audience)* I'm being punished. Can you believe it? Seventeen years old, and I'm stuck on the couch like a child. It's ridiculous. I'm surprised she didn't make me sit in the corner or something.

Parents. I ask you . . . do they have any idea what they're doing? Mom has 10 books about dealing with an adolescent—that's me, by the way. The adolescent. My voice started to change, and she panicked. She went straight to the Christian bookstore and grabbed those books. She wasn't taking any chances. *(Pause)* The only time Mom ever uses those books is when she needs something to hit me with.

Sometimes I just can't figure her out. I slept in this morning. I mean, it's Saturday, right? So I decided to sleep late. No big deal. You think she'd be grateful. When I was four, I used to jump on her at 6 a.m., and she'd always tell me to go back to bed. So now I'm 17; I'm finally taking her advice, and she rips into my room like the white tornado . . . screaming at me to get out of bed. She's talking non-stop as she tears open my curtains.

(With mother's voice) "Look at this pigsty. I've never seen anything like it. You should be ashamed to sleep in a mess like this. How can you stand it? Get out of that bed this instant! Is this how you're going to live your life—messing up rooms and sleeping all day?"

(In his own voice) And I said, "Good morning, Mom."

Then she said, *(With a mother's voice)* "Don't get smart

with me, young man."

(Himself) And I know it's going to be one of those days.

(With mother's voice) "What's all this garbage? How can you possibly manufacture such a large amount of garbage in one room? I swear you must sneak it in here, during the middle of the night when your father and I are asleep."

(Himself) Right, Mom.

(With mother's voice) "Did you say something?"

(Himself) No, Mom.

And then Dad made the mistake of coming in to ask me if I had the keys to the car. Normally, he wouldn't come near my room when Mom's there, but it must have been an emergency—like trying to get out of the house before Mom turned on *him*. Too late.

(With mother's voice) "Look at this room, Henry. Do you *see* this room?"

(Himself) And Dad said, *(With father's voice)* "Uh-huh . . . Son, do you have the keys to the . . ."

(With mother's voice) " 'Uh-huh?' Is that all you can say? 'Uh-huh.' This place looks like a toxic waste dump, and that's all you can say?"

(With father's voice) "Uh-huh."

(With mother's voice) "Just what I'd expect. Like father, like son. He inherited his knack for clutter from *you*."

(Himself) I said, "Mom, I'll clean it up as soon as I . . ."

(With mother's voice) "Don't argue with me! I want you to clean it up *this minute*! Both of you think I'm nothing but your housekeeper, don't you? Well, I'm *not*."

(Himself) Then Dad said, *(With father's voice)* "I never said you're just a housekeeper."

(With mother's voice) "Not in words, Henry. But actions speak louder than words!"

(Himself) This woman is a walking thesaurus of quotations.

(With mother's voice) "Why do I even have to *tell* you to clean your room? Why don't you take some initiative yourself? If your life is going to be like this room, you're in big trouble. Do you hear me? You're just like your father."

(With father's voice) "Now, hold on just a minute here."

(With mother's voice) "I'm sick to death of the both of you. For a nickel I'd join a convent and leave you two to wallow in your messes."

(Himself) I gave her a nickel off of my dresser. That was *my* mistake. Dad laughed out loud. That was *his* mistake.

I'd tell you the rest but . . . well, the violence would give this story an R rating. It was gruesome—a terror to behold! There was no saving me, the day I was born, my father, the day they were married or the worst habits of all his relatives . . . who were named one by one. It was absolute carnage!

So here I am. She wants me to stay in here and think about *(With mother's voice)* "watching my mouth in the future." *(Himself)* A beautiful Saturday, and I have to sit here and think about my mouth.

Dad's punishment is worse. He has to clean out the attic—a job he's been putting off for 13 years. It's not a pretty sight. I don't know if we'll recover.

MOTHER   *(From offstage)* Come in here, David! Your father needs help moving some boxes!

DAVID   *(To the audience)* No, we may not recover at all. *(Slowly stands and walks off to pay his penance)*

The end.

. . . .

Discussion Questions

1. This *exact* situation might not seem familiar. But which elements in this sketch remind you of your home? Explain.

2. We seem to live in an age of "how-to" books, films and videos about family behavior. Do you have any of these forms of communication in your home? Do such influences make a difference in how you relate to your parents and how they relate to you?

3. Despite all the practical advice we receive about making family relationships better, we're all still human—with varying moods and quirks. How "moody" are your family members? your mother? your father? your brothers and sisters? you? How do you respond to your family members' moods? How do you expect your family members to respond to *your* moods?

4. Have you ever had a time when you were unreasonable about something—in your words or actions? What happened? What causes such times?

5. Do you think a 17-year-old should be made to sit on the couch as a punishment? If a parent needs to punish a teenager, what's the most effective way to do it? What's the most effective punishment for *you*?

6. Read Exodus 20:12 and Ephesians 6:1-4. How do these scripture passages apply to your relationships with your parents?

Father and Son

Preparation

Rather than beginning with a warm-up, start by having everyone answer the question, "What's the worst thing you've ever done?" Make sure everyone in the group responds, no exceptions.

The relationship between a father and son often determines how a son chooses a career, relates to other people (even a girlfriend or a wife) and, most importantly, feels about himself. This sketch examines conflict and lack of communication between a father and his son. Encourage girls each to think about their relationship with their father as they watch this sketch.

Characters

FATHER
SON

Setting

A living room
A few chairs

(Father enters looking disheveled. He's wearing a shirt that's buttoned with the wrong holes, pants that don't match, a bathrobe and slippers. The son follows, also looking disheveled, and plops down in a chair)

FATHER   *(With his back to son, speaks angrily)* I want you to sit—

SON   I am.

FATHER   —down. What am I going to do with you? What *am* I going to do with you?

SON   I give up. What are you going to do with me?

FATHER   I should have left you in jail.

SON   Yeah! That woulda taught me a lesson.

FATHER   It would have, young man. I should take you back.

SON   How about if I have a few more drinks and get arrested for drunk driving again? The police could save you a trip.

FATHER   Are you trying to be funny?

SON   Oh, no sir. I'm quite serious.

FATHER   You're not funny.

SON   *(Looks at his watch, reacts dramatically)* Look at this!

FATHER   Yes, it's 2:30 in the morning.

SON   No—I scratched the crystal. I must've bumped it on the steering wheel when I swerved to miss that tree that jumped in front of me.

FATHER   You're really trying to be funny, aren't you? Well, this *isn't* funny!

SON   You're telling me. I paid big bucks for this watch.

FATHER   Forget the watch . . . I'm talking about *you*, young man. Drunk driving—a near accident—bailing you out of jail. None of this is funny at all. What am I going to do with you? Huh? Huh?

(Son doesn't answer but finally shrugs his shoulders)

FATHER   Why? *Why* do you do this?

SON   Gee, Pop. Maybe it's something deeply psychological. Maybe I should see a therapist or get shock treatments.

FATHER   Maybe I should lock you in the closet until you decide to straighten up. I'd give you a spanking if I thought it would do any good.

SON   What makes you so sure it won't? You're pretty good at the physical stuff.

FATHER   What's that supposed to mean?

SON   Oh, you know—push me around—hit me in the arm a few times—jab me in the stomach when I'm not expecting it. All that *manly* kind of stuff you do.

FATHER   You're still drunk. I don't know what you're talking about.

SON   Let's arm-wrestle, Dad. Come on. *(Positions himself to do it)*

FATHER   Forget it. You're drunk.

SON   *(Stays in position)* Come on. Arm-wrestle with me . . . like we used to.

FATHER   I'll have an unfair advantage.

SON   Nothing new.

FATHER   I don't know what you're talking about.

SON   You probably don't. *(Pause)* Come on . . . a quickie.

FATHER   This is stupid. *(Positions himself opposite his son and takes his hand to arm-wrestle)*

SON   Whenever you're ready.

FATHER   One . . . two . . . three . . .

(Both go at it; doesn't take long for the father to beat the son)

SON   *(With sarcastic enthusiasm)* What a victory.

FATHER   You didn't try.

SON   How would you know?

FATHER   You didn't. I don't know why I let you talk me into that. It's the middle of the night. *(Shakes a finger at him)* Don't think this lets you off the hook.

SON   Never. I'm still waiting for your decision.

FATHER   What decision?

SON   What you're going to do with me . . . this failure of a son.

FATHER   I don't know.

SON   Be honest, Pop. What do you *want* to do with me—or *to* me? Kick me across the room? Scream and yell at me? Leave me in a basket on someone's doorstep?

FATHER   All of the above. Why are you doing this—huh?

SON   The name's Billy—not "huh."

FATHER   Why do you act like this? I get you a nice car, and you abuse it. Everything I give you, you abuse. This is the thanks I get. Other kids would *kill* to live your life. I gave you everything.

SON   You gave me everything. Is that what you said—*everything*?

FATHER   You know it.

SON   The only reason you gave me *everything*, my dear father, was to keep me out of your hair. Take this toy, Billy, and go in the other room. Take this money, Billy, and go see a movie. Take this car, Billy, and go anywhere but where I am.

FATHER   You don't know what you're talking about.

SON   Why didn't you give me something I didn't have to *leave* to enjoy?

FATHER   This is crazy. Like *what*, huh?

SON   Like your love maybe.

FATHER   This is a *stupid* conversation. Go to bed and sleep it off. *(Pause)* What am I gonna do with you?

SON   You never knew. *(Pause)* Goodbye, Dad. *(Exits)*

FATHER   Hey—where you going? Come back here! *(Moves to the door)* Billy! *(Waves him off)* Ah—the police'll get him again. Let 'em leave that spoiled brat in jail.

(Moves across the room to go to bed, flexes his arm-wrestling hand, then stops with a sudden look of emotion. Turns to where Billy exited) Billy! *(Exits in that direction)*

The end.

. . . .

Discussion Questions

1. What was wrong with the relationship between Billy and his father? How could these problems be corrected? Do you think Billy left for good, or will he come back?

2. Read Proverbs 3:12; 4:1; and Ephesians 6:4. What relationship do these scripture passages suggest for a father and son relationship? What's required of the son? the father?

3. What do you appreciate most about your relationship with *your* father? How do you think it could be improved on his part? your part?

4. How does your father *show* his love—for you and other members of your family?

5. What makes you angriest with your father? What do you do that makes him angry with you?

6. Is there anything in your life that you've never forgiven your father for? Is there anything in your life that your father needs to forgive *you* for?

7. What have you wanted to ask your father but haven't? Why haven't you asked?

8. What one thing have you always wanted to say to your father but haven't? What's prevented you from saying it?

9. What one thing have you always wanted to hear your father say to you, but he hasn't? What do you think has stopped him from saying it?

Topic: *Low self-esteem*

Bad Day at School

Preparation

Start with Warm-Up #1 (page 11) or #17 (page 21).

This monologue works two ways. It looks at the alienation felt by an individual who sees himself as different from others. It also examines feelings of dislike for one's own personality and the desire to change. As an interesting twist, have someone totally unlike the character of Steve—a popular student or jock—play this part.

Characters

STEVE—a stereotypical nerd who's struggling with his differences

Setting

Steve's bedroom (Can be as simple or as elaborate as you want—or just an empty stage)

. . . .

(Steve enters. He is, in all senses of the word, a nerd, geek or whatever expression is being used for such stereotypes)

STEVE   I didn't have a very good day at school today. I mean, most of the time I don't have good days at school, but today was less good than most. It's not that I have problems with school *per se*—that's Latin by the way—I'm trilingual. *(Pauses)* I also speak three languages. *(He laughs heartily at his little joke)* That was a little joke. You see, trilingual means . . . oh, never mind. I crack myself up sometimes.

See, most of the time I don't mind them picking on me. You know, they knock my books out of my hands and hit me in the back of the head over and over when I'm trying to pick up the papers. They call me names like pizza-face and lizard-lips and one or two that I can't repeat—especially since I don't know what they mean. They put things in my gym shorts that make my eyes water. And sometimes they put rude things in the chemicals we use for Science Club.

Mom says they're jealous of me because I'm smart. I used to believe her. But then she said that they were jealous because of my physique. *(Pauses; tries some typical body-builder poses to show off his physique)* She was lying to me. But it doesn't matter.

(Smiling) I became a Christian a little while ago. I go to church a lot now. The teenagers there don't knock my books out of my hands or call me names. Most of the time they just ignore me. *(Pauses, confused)* I don't know which is worse.

I read in the Bible that God would make me "a new creation." I wish he'd get started. I'm ready for him to make me into something else—into someone that people will like.

I've been thinking of submitting some requests to him about who I want to be . . . maybe someone from the Bible, you know? Those guys were neat, and people looked up to them. You know who I'm talking about. *(Thinks for a moment)* I wouldn't mind being somebody like . . . oh, Samson maybe. He was big and strong—and had all kinds of women hanging around him. *(Pause)* Well, maybe not. He was okay as a barbell boy, but he wasn't very smart when it came to getting his hair styled—if you know what I mean.

(Thinks about it more) King David! Yeah, he was cool. He

was valiant, a "man after God's own heart," he won all those battles and . . . *(Not so enthused as he remembers)* committed adultery and murder. Even his own son turned against him. Hmmm . . . okay, so David had problems too. Who else?

(Thinks even more) Solomon, maybe? They said he was the wisest man who ever lived. But . . . he had all those wives and concubines . . . and wrote those proverbs and that book that says everything is futile and vain and . . . well, maybe not.

(Thinks again) The Apostle Paul! I'd like to be like him. A powerful man of God, leading all kinds of people to Christ and healing the sick and . . . and . . . *(Pause)* shipwrecked, nearly murdered, put in jail, beaten and . . .

(Ponders more) All right . . . so maybe those guys had problems too. But, hey, they had God on their side. He helped them. All I have is . . . *(Pauses as he realizes)* . . . God. *(Further realization)* Maybe that's the idea. Maybe that's what made those guys so special, y' know? It wasn't who they were or who picked on them but how they let God handle their problems. I'm gonna have to think about that. There might be hope for me yet . . .

Oh well. At least tomorrow's Saturday. That gives God a couple of days to prepare me for Monday. Besides, this is the weekend I get to help Mom scrape the barnacles off the fishbowl.

My life's not so bad, I guess. *(Exits)*

The end.

. . . .

Discussion Questions

1. You probably know someone like Steve. How do you feel about him? How do you react to someone like him?

2. Steve says that he gets picked on in school. At church, however, kids don't pick on him; youth group members simply ignore him. He wonders, "Which is worse?" How would you respond to the concern expressed in his question?

3. Steve also wishes he could be like someone else. Have you ever wished that? If so, who would you want to be like? Select one person or attributes from several people, and give reasons for your selection.

4. List things you don't like in other people's personalities. Now make a second list of things you don't like in *your* personality. Compare the two lists. Are there similarities? What are they? Are there differences? Describe them. Have you discovered anything new from these two lists? If so, what?

5. What was Steve's conclusion to wanting to change his personality? Do you agree with him? Can you relate to his conclusion? If so, how?

6. Steve says he wants to be a new creation. Read 2 Corinthians 5:17. What does this scripture passage mean to you? What's "old" in your life? What's "new"? Be specific. What is God's prerequisite for becoming a new creation? For more information about becoming a new creation, read and discuss the following scripture passages: Romans 3:23; 5:8; 6:23; 10:9-13; and John 3:16.

Topic: *Mother and daughter relationships*

The Return

Preparation

Start with Warm-Up #5 (page 13), #9 (page 17) or #7 (page 14).

The sketch examines a mother and daughter's attempts to heal a relationship that's been severed. The attempts to heal the relationship include open and honest communication from both people. Encourage guys each to think about their relationship with their mother as they watch this sketch.

Characters

BRENDA—the daughter who's left home and returned
BEV—Brenda's mother

Setting

Their living room

- - - - - - - - - - - - - - - - -

(Brenda walks into the room and stops for a moment. Pushing aside any feelings, she moves in and wanders casually about the room. Bev, her mother, enters. There's definite tension, even awkwardness, about this encounter)

BEV   You're home. What a surprise. I mean, we didn't know the exact time you'd come back. *(Pauses as if waiting for something—an explanation perhaps. When Brenda says nothing, she continues)*

I just talked to your father on the phone. He's coming right home from the office. He doesn't usually do that, you know. But tonight—he's coming straight home. *(Another pause, as if waiting for a response. Again, she has to continue)*

I don't want to be pushy—I'm not being pushy at all— but it would be nice if you could stay for dinner. You don't have to if you don't want—but it would be nice. You could even stay for more than just dinner if you want. *(Pause)*

Your room is exactly as you left it. *(Pause, chuckles nervously)* Well, not *exactly*. I did have to throw away the cheese sandwich you left under the bed. What I mean is that the room is there if you want to stay in it tonight . . . or tomorrow night . . . or as many nights as you want.

BRENDA Mom . . .

BEV *(Nervously)* I'm being pushy, aren't I? Your father just said on the phone, "Now, Bev, don't be pushy. She's been gone for an entire summer, and you don't want to be pushy." So I'm trying very hard not to be pushy because your father doesn't want me to *(Bordering on tears)* drive you away again.

(Trying to control herself) I'm sorry. I'm sorry. It's just been a long three months. *(Long pause; a second attempt to gain more control)* But it's all right. I won't be pushy. We don't have to talk about it. We don't have to talk about anything.

BRENDA Mom . . .

(Bev looks at her silently)

BRENDA It's tough. I know it's tough. I'm not even sure why I'm here.

BEV That's all right. Really, it's all right. You don't have to say anymore.

BRENDA   There hasn't been a whole lot of love lost between us. We both know that. There's no point in pretending.

BEV   You're a very independent person, Brenda. I know that now. I've been studying . . . reading. I want to say the right things. I really do . . . like your father. He always says the right things. That's why he wants me to keep my mouth shut until he gets home.

BRENDA   This is between us, Mom.

BEV   Yes, it is. But when your father gets here, he'll say the right things. I'm still trying to learn. I am. I don't want to fight with you anymore. I don't want to drive you away.

BRENDA   I don't know if . . . well, whether or not I'm moving back in.

BEV   No, of course not. Not if you don't want to.

BRENDA   But I'll be living in the area.

BEV   Good. Good. You can visit. *(Quick pause)* No, you don't have to visit. *(Self-consciously)* I'm being pushy again. You can do what you want.

BRENDA   I want to start over with you. I'd like to . . . to be friends again. Remember when we were friends?

BEV   I remember.

BRENDA   I used to tell you everything.

BEV   I don't know what happened.

BRENDA   I don't either. Something changed. I changed. We can work at it.

BEV   Yes, I suppose we can. I don't know how something like that works, but we can try. I've been reading . . . studying . . .

BRENDA   To say the right things.

BEV   To say the right things *because I never seem to*. You know I remember hearing myself talking to you. It's like I was always yelling at the top of my lungs . . . always yelling. What was I yelling? What was I saying? Never the right things. And then you went away and . . . the house echoed. All the right things I never said echoed all over the house. Then I realized what it was I never said . . . but then it was too late.

BRENDA We'll work on it, Mom.

BEV I just assumed you knew, Brenda. I never thought I needed to say it. I told you once when you fell off your bicycle and skinned your knee. But that's the only time I can remember.

BRENDA Mom, I don't know what you're talking about.

BEV You don't? That's because I'm rambling. I ramble a lot. That's why I have so much trouble. I ramble instead of just *saying it*.

BRENDA Saying it? Saying *what*?

BEV I . . . I love you, Brenda.

BRENDA *(Confused)* What?

BEV I just assumed you always knew, and I was wrong. I love you. There . . . that's not so hard. You don't have to say anything. Maybe it would be better if you didn't. We can work on it. It just seemed like the best place to start.

(Speechless and obviously moved, Brenda embraces her mother)

BEV I did all right, then? I didn't say the wrong thing?

BRENDA *(Through her tears)* No. You said just the right thing.

(They hold tightly to each other. After a few moments they hear a car door slam)

BEV Let's say "hello" to your father. *(They exit with their arms around each other's waists)*

The end.

. . . .

Discussion Questions

1. What seemed to be wrong with the relationship between Brenda and her mother? How could it be corrected? Do you think Brenda will move home again? Why or why not?

2. What do you appreciate most about your relationship with *your* mother? How do you think it could be improved on her part? your part?

3. How does your mother show her love for you? for the rest of your family members?

4. What makes you angriest with your mother? What do you do that makes her angry with you?

5. Is there anything in your life that you've never forgiven your mother for? Is there anything in your life your mother needs to forgive *you* for?

6. What have you wanted to ask your mother but haven't? Why haven't you asked?

7. What one thing have you always wanted to say to your mother but haven't? What's prevented you from saying it?

8. What one thing have you always wanted to hear your mother say to you, but she hasn't? What do you think has stopped her from saying it?

9. This sketch seems to end happily, but was it realistic? Read Luke 15:11-25. Bev was excited about Brenda's return and was finally able to tell her daughter that she loves her. But is that enough to overcome their differences? How would you advise them to proceed from this point?

Topic: *Obedience to God/Attitudes*

A Fleeting Moment

Preparation

Start with Warm-Up #11 (page 18), #16 (page 20) or #24 (page 27).

In this sketch a young person deals with his convictions. The sketch explores a family's (and in a broader sense, society's) reactions to such convictions. This sketch could be done in a "readers theater" style.

Characters

SON
FATHER
MOTHER
DAUGHTER

Setting

A blank stage

(Characters should perform this sketch motionless, using only their voices to convey any emotions implied by the lines)

SON   It was a fleeting moment . . . a sudden lapse of priorities.

DAUGHTER   Who's been using my curling iron?!

SON   I'm not exactly sure where the idea came from. It may have been buried inside of me—just waiting for the right circumstances to come alive. Maybe the minister's sermon was the right circumstance.

MOTHER   If we budget properly, we might be able to have our pool built by next summer.

SON   That sermon made me think about life. Sometimes I get the feeling I'm missing something.

DAUGHTER   Hey! I'm watching that program! Turn it back!

SON   The minister was talking about people living in poverty.

FATHER   Someone scratched the paint on the car.

SON   I don't think I know what that is—poverty.

DAUGHTER   Mom, I saw a beautiful bracelet with matching earrings in the catalog.

SON   I've read about it, but I've never seen it. We don't believe in poverty anyway . . . at least, not as a rule.

MOTHER   We went to Le Château for lunch. I can write it off as a tax deduction.

SON   People starving. Little kids with big eyes and bloated stomachs.

FATHER   Get a *real* job.

SON   And then the minister talked about missions . . . how they need help.

FATHER   I tithe. Why are they always asking for more money?

SON   People aren't only dying . . . they're dying without Christ.

DAUGHTER	Did you see that dress she was wearing? How embarrassing!
SON	These people don't know about Jesus. Christians have stopped going into the mission field.
MOTHER	Where are the car keys? I'm late for my meeting.
SON	The minister challenged us to pray about going into missions.
FATHER	This high-yield certificate might be a very good investment.
SON	So I thought I would volunteer.
MOTHER, FATHER, DAUGHTER	What?!?! *(Turning and looking at the son in disbelief)*
MOTHER	Think of the sacrifices.
FATHER	Think of the finances.
DAUGHTER	Think of the kind of people you'll be dealing with—or the clothes you'll have to wear.
FATHER	What will other people think?
MOTHER	What will our friends say?
DAUGHTER	It's just another phase.
MOTHER	Don't be silly.
FATHER	I'll send another check. It'll do more than you will.
SON	It was just a thought.
FATHER	It's just an emotional reaction.
SON	It was a fleeting moment . . . a sudden lapse of priorities.
MOTHER	Jesus wasn't talking literally.
SON	I'm thinking much clearer now. *(Pause, sadly)* It won't happen again.

The end.

. . . .

Discussion Questions

1. List ways we determine God's will for our lives. (For example, through reading the Bible, listening to sermons, evaluating our impressions and feelings, and receiving advice from friends or family.)

2. Identify times in your life when you felt you should do something God wanted you to do, but *didn't* do it. Explain what prevented you from taking action.

3. Identify times in your life when you felt like you should do something God wanted you to do and *did* it. What prompted you to follow through? How were these times different from those when you didn't act?

4. What prevents people from doing what God wants them to do? Read Romans 7:15, 19-20. Explain how this scripture passage applies to you.

5. Discuss what should happen if you *know* God wants you to do something, but you don't *feel* it. What's the difference? Should you act apart from your feelings, or must feelings always be a prerequisite to action? For example, should you go to church even if you don't *feel* like it? Read 1 John 2:3-6. How does that scripture passage affect your answer?

6. Locate your church's mission statement and read it. Is there anyone in your group who has considered going into the mission field? What was his or her final decision? Why?

Topic: *Peer pressure*

The Choice

Preparation

Start with Warm-Up #7 (page 14), #14 (page 20) or #22 (page 26).
Even though this sketch seems absurd, it explores the issue of peer pressure as Robin offers Kelly a stick of gum. Guys can play either or both parts.

Characters

ROBIN—the gum chewer
KELLY—the person who doesn't want to chew gum

Setting

Any informal setting
Two chairs

. . . .

(Robin and Kelly casually walk to the chairs and sit down)

ROBIN *(Reaches into pocket, pulls out a stick of gum, unwraps it and pops it in mouth. Reaches in for another stick and offers it to Kelly)* Gum?

KELLY No thanks.

ROBIN Whatdaya mean "no thanks"? It's gum.

KELLY Yeah. I recognize it. But no thanks.

ROBIN It's good gum.

KELLY I believe you.

ROBIN Then why don't you want some?

KELLY I don't chew gum.

ROBIN Whatdaya mean you don't chew gum?

KELLY Just what I said. I'm not interested.

ROBIN How could you not be interested—it's *gum*. Have some.

KELLY No thanks.

ROBIN I don't believe you.

KELLY Huh?

ROBIN What's wrong with gum?

KELLY Nothing, I guess. I just don't like it.

ROBIN *Why* don't you like it?

KELLY I don't know. I just never have. And besides, it's . . . bad for my teeth.

ROBIN Bad for your teeth? Breathing is bad for your lungs. *Everything's* bad for you these days. *(Holds the stick of gum toward Kelly again)* Here, have some gum.

KELLY I don't want any gum. It hurts my jaw to chew gum.

ROBIN That's because you haven't done it enough. If you chewed more gum, you'd get used to it.

KELLY I don't want to get used to it.

ROBIN But . . . it's gum! It's got a great taste!

KELLY It's okay.

ROBIN It makes you look good . . . *feel* good.

KELLY That's what the commercials say. I don't know if I believe it.

ROBIN This is weird . . . totally weird.

KELLY What's so weird?

ROBIN You not chewing gum. Uncool, Kelly, really uncool.

KELLY Uncool?

ROBIN Yeah. Barbara said you were like this, but I didn't want to believe her.

KELLY Barbara? What's Barbara got to do with this?

ROBIN When's the last time you were invited to a party?

KELLY *(Thinking)* It's been a while. But I've been busy.

ROBIN Uh-huh. And you haven't been dating much either.

KELLY No. But that's because . . .

ROBIN You've been busy. Right?

KELLY Wait. You're saying that I don't get invited to parties or asked out on dates because I don't chew gum?

ROBIN Nobody likes to *say* it.

KELLY *(Pondering what was said)* I didn't realize . . .

ROBIN Kelly, if you wanna be on the inside track, you gotta run with the right crowd. Do what they do . . .

KELLY Chew what they chew.

ROBIN Now you got it. Unless, of course, you don't *want* to be part of the group. I'm sure there are people *somewhere* who agree with you about gum-chewing. You never see much of them though—except at geek activities.

KELLY You really think it's that important?

ROBIN It speaks for itself. Look around. Who do you want to be like?

(Kelly silently considers this for a moment)

ROBIN *(Holds gum out)* Want some gum?

(Stop sketch here and talk about questions)

The end.

. . . .

Discussion Questions

1. How should Kelly react? Should Kelly take the gum? Why or why not?

2. Talk about other peer pressure issues such as clothing, hair styles, choosing friends, academic achievement, drinking, drugs, "how far to go" on a date, sex or religion. With each issue, list the consequences for conforming with the crowd and the consequences for *not* conforming.

3. How should Christians react to peer pressure—particularly with the topics you discussed in the previous question? The personal religious beliefs of Robin and Kelly aren't stated. Speculate what they might be, and explain why you think as you do. Based on your speculation, answer question 1 again.

4. Read John 12:43; Romans 12:2; 1 Peter 2:5, 9-10; and 1 John 2:15-17. What do these scripture passages say about peer pressure? How would you put them into practice in your personal encounters with others? Be specific.

Topic: *Physical and emotional abuse*

Misunderstood

Preparation

Start with Warm-Up #6 (page 14) or #8 (page 15).

There's a certain amount of shock value to this monologue. It might be best to have someone, preferably an adult male, memorize or practice reading this monologue before performing it for the group.

Caution for the leader: Because of the nature of this monologue and the following discussion questions, do research about abuse ahead of time, and know what direction you want to go with the young people's questions. Be prepared to help or refer possible (and previously unknown) victims of abuse. Don't assume you know about treating these people's unique needs unless you're profession-ally trained to do so.

Characters

A MAN

Setting

A living room, or some place where a person would go to be alone
A chair

(The man enters, nervous and anxious. He paces for a moment then addresses the audience as if it were another person in the room)

MAN   *(Pacing around the room like a lion in a cage)* I don't understand. I don't understand at all. They shouldn't be allowed to do this to me. It isn't right. I work hard. I pay my taxes. Who are they to invade my home, huh? It isn't right.

A man should be master in his own castle. I believe that's in the Bible. Well, maybe it wasn't a "castle" back then. A tent. King of his own tent. *I* pay the bills. *I* make the decisions. It's *my* role, *my* responsibility—*my burden. (Pauses and sits down)*

Yeah, my *burden.* Folks don't think about that much—the burden of being provider, husband *and* father. Twenty-four hours a day! Let me tell you. I work hard all day. When I come home, is it too much to ask that the house be picked up? Huh? Maybe the toys aren't under my feet? Or maybe there's some peace and quiet?

But there she is—in a dirty housedress. The kids are fighting, and she says *I* gotta make a decision. Spare the rod and spoil the child, you know? I gotta administer a little discipline. That's my role, my responsibility—my burden.

(Stands and starts pacing again) I don't like it. I don't like to do it, but I *have* to. Understand? I have to *hit* 'em to get 'em under control. It's like . . . they *expect* it. They *want* it.

And what do they think's gonna happen? Huh? Sometimes a black eye. Sometimes a cut. Okay, a broken bone looks bad . . . but it's the risk of solid discipline. Can I help it? It's not like I *enjoy* it, but, y' know, they get me so *mad.*

I don't lose control . . . not ever. They're just a little more fragile than I was when I was growing up . . . *when my dad hit me. (Pauses)*

I don't understand. They're my *babies.* I wouldn't hurt 'em on purpose. They don't have to take 'em away from me. They don't . . . *(Appears ready to cry, but instead straightens and composes himself)* The problem is that no one understands. They just don't understand. *(Exits)*

The end.
. . . .

Discussion Questions

1. How do you feel about this man? Why? What do you think should happen to him? Why?

2. Do you know any individuals who've been abused? If so, how are they dealing with their abuse? How have you been able to help (if you're in a position to do so)?

3. Do you suspect anyone of being a child or spouse abuser? What makes you think so? What, if anything, should you do about it?

4. What's the most effective means of discipline for children who disobey? What do you think of physical punishment as a form of discipline for raising children?

5. Read Matthew 9:12-13. How does this scripture passage apply to the abused? the abuser? the church? you?

The Test

Preparation

Start with Warm-Up #1 (page 11), #7 (page 14) or #20 (page 25).

Before this sketch, ask different young people to read aloud the following verses to your group: Matthew 7:7; 18:19; 21:21-22; John 14:14; and 1 John 3:22. To help your discussion, explain that this sketch has two messages: attitudes toward prayer and preparing for tests. Roles may be played by either gender.

Characters

CHRIS—the person who hasn't studied and is depending on God to help pass the test

KELLY—the friend who's studied for the test

Setting

A school library
A table
Two chairs

(Kelly is seated. Chris enters anxiously and sits down next to Kelly)

KELLY Hi, Chris.

CHRIS I don't want to talk about it.

KELLY Talk about what? I said "hi."

CHRIS Oh, hi. Have you seen Mrs. Campbell? Is she sick today?

KELLY No. I saw her earlier. What's wrong with you?

CHRIS We're taking a test today—that's what's wrong with me.

KELLY Yeah. So?

CHRIS So! Did you say, "So!"?

KELLY So . . . you're not ready for it?

CHRIS Ready? *(Giggles on the verge of psychotic hysteria)* What makes you think I'm not ready?

KELLY Are you?

CHRIS No . . . but it's okay. It's all right. Everything will be just fine.

KELLY Really? Did you study a lot?

CHRIS Study? Maybe a little bit. I . . . I started watching a movie on TV, and . . . the night just slipped away from me.

KELLY You didn't study at *all*?

CHRIS It's okay. It's all right. Everything will be just fine.

KELLY Wow. You must know this stuff pretty good. I had to study the whole night. What do you do—study a little bit every night to make sure you know it?

CHRIS No.

KELLY Then why do you think everything's going to be all right? I mean, this test is gonna determine your final grade in the class!

CHRIS I know that. You don't think I know that?

KELLY Then . . . ?

CHRIS 'Cause I prayed about it. Real hard. This morning.

KELLY You prayed?

CHRIS   Yeah. If God really loves me, he won't let me fail this exam.

KELLY   Does it work like that?

CHRIS   It better. It *has* to or I'm in *big* trouble.

KELLY   No kidding. For your sake, I hope it does.

CHRIS   It will. I had to do the same thing for a test I took last week.

KELLY   Did you pass?

CHRIS   No. But I think God deserves a second chance.

KELLY   Wouldn't it make more sense to *study*?

CHRIS   Yeah. But that takes a lot of work. I'm a person of *faith*, not *works*.

KELLY   I think you're out of your mind.

CHRIS   *(Feeling panicked again)* I think so too. I feel the need to pray coming on again. *(Puts head down and spreads arms to heavens)* Oh help me, help me, help me, help me. My parents are gonna kill me, kill me, kill me.

KELLY   Chris—we gotta go. It's time for class. *(Begins pulling Chris off stage)*

CHRIS   Please, please, please, please . . . *(Stops)*

KELLY   Quickly, where did the Continental Congress meet to discuss independence from Great Britain?

CHRIS   Ummm . . . Cleveland?

KELLY   Keep praying. *(Continues to drag Chris off stage)*

CHRIS   *(Praying as they exit)* Help me, help me, help me, help me. *(Both exit)*

The end.

. . . .

Discussion Questions

1. Re-examine the Bible verses read at the beginning. Interpret them first in their context and then in light of your personal experiences with prayer.

2. According to these verses, was Chris within his or her "rights" to expect God's help on the test? Why or why not? Under what circumstances can we expect God to answer our prayers? Explain.

3. Why do you pray? What do you pray hardest for? Does God answer your prayers? How do you react when he does? when he doesn't?

4. What was Chris' fundamental problem with preparing for this test? How could Chris have avoided this situation? How do you prepare for tests? Would you say your method of preparation is effective? Why or why not? How might it be improved?

5. Apart from taking tests, can you think of a time you got in a "jam" because of your own doing and asked God to bail you out? What happened? What do you imagine God was thinking during this time?

6. Read Matthew 25:1-12. What happened to the maidens who weren't prepared? Find other scriptural examples of people who got into trouble because of their own doing and called upon God. What happened to them?

Topic: *Sibling tension*

Sisters

Preparation

Start with Warm-Up #1 (page 11), #16 (page 20) or #25 (page 27).

This sketch explores the tension that often exists between siblings—in this case, two sisters.

Characters

ELIZABETH—the sister who feels her mother favors her sister

RUTH—the sister who seems to be favored

Setting

Any room in the house

- - - - - - - - - - - - - - - -

(Elizabeth storms on stage. Ruth follows)

ELIZABETH Don't follow me. Just *don't* follow me. I want to be left alone.

RUTH You hate me, don't you? Why do you hate me?

ELIZABETH You want to know? You *really* want to know?

RUTH Yes.

ELIZABETH	Because you exist.
RUTH	I can't help it.
ELIZABETH	Yes, you can. Run away from home.
RUTH	No! Why should I?
ELIZABETH	I thought you wanted to help.
RUTH	What's wrong with you?
ELIZABETH	I'm sick and tired of you being Mom's favorite daughter.
RUTH	*What?*
ELIZABETH	Oh, don't play all innocent and sweet like you don't know what I'm talking about. You know. You eat it up.
RUTH	You're dreaming.
ELIZABETH	Dreaming—a nightmare! You're Cinderella and I'm all three ugly sisters. Everything you do is perfect . . . what you wear . . . what you say . . . what you think. Mom loves it.
RUTH	That's not true.
ELIZABETH	You could punch her in the face and she'd think it was the best thing in the world.
RUTH	That's *not* true!
ELIZABETH	No? Her last birthday—remember?
RUTH	Yes, I remember. What about it?
ELIZABETH	I spent *days* looking for a gift. I tried everywhere. I finally got her some of that perfume she likes. Big bucks for that little bottle—and how did she react when I gave it to her? "Oh, how nice." Then she shoved it in her dresser drawer and hasn't touched it since.
RUTH	Her taste in perfume changed.
ELIZABETH	So did her interior decorating skills. *You* bought her a cheesy 50 cent birthday card, and it's *still* sitting on the mantelpiece in the living room. She showed it to *everybody*. It was so "cuuuuuute"—her little birthday

card from her "snookie-ookums baby daughter." .

RUTH It's not my fault.

ELIZABETH Yes it is. .

RUTH Why?

ELIZABETH Because you *exist*!

RUTH Aren't you being a little overdramatic?

ELIZABETH What just happened at the dinner table? I tried to tell her about my day . . . my speech at the student council meeting, the A I got on my math test, my award for academic excellence. And what was her response?

RUTH I don't remember.

ELIZABETH Of course you don't remember! There wasn't any! She asked me to pass the salt! All of that—and I'm a spice courier. Wonder what she'd have me do if I won the Nobel Peace Prize—pour her some water? And *you*!

RUTH What?

ELIZABETH You mentioned that you learned a new chord during your piano lessons, and Mom acted like you'd played to a standing-room audience at Carnegie Hall!

RUTH I can't help it. What am I supposed to do?

ELIZABETH I told you—

RUTH I'm *not* running away from home.

ELIZABETH Then give me at least a fighting chance! Mess up once or twice!

RUTH How?

ELIZABETH Call Mom a dirty name.

RUTH I can't do that.

ELIZABETH Don't clean your room until she tells you.

RUTH Ahhh . . .

ELIZABETH Bring home someone really scuzzy and say you're getting married.

RUTH   No way.

ELIZABETH   Don't shave your armpits for a month. I don't care. Just stop being so perfect. And maybe—*(Voice becomes sadly quiet)*—just maybe—in that moment when she realizes that you're not perfect, she'll realize that *I* don't have to be perfect either. Maybe then she'll remember that I'm her daughter too.

RUTH   *(Trying to comfort)* Elizabeth . . .

ELIZABETH   No. Don't say anything. I'm sure it'll be just the right thing, and I'll resent you for it.

RUTH   What can I do? I can't be anything less than what I am.

ELIZABETH   *(Long pause, realizing the truth of her statement)* No, I guess you're right.

RUTH   Then, what . . . what can I do? You're my sister. I don't like the idea that you hate me.

ELIZABETH   *(Pauses)* I don't really hate you. I want to . . . but I can't.

RUTH   Then what'll we do?

ELIZABETH   We? No . . . me. *(Pauses to think about the answer, then shrugs)* I'll go help Mom with the dishes. Maybe the shock will do some good. *(Moves to exit)*

RUTH   Elizabeth . . .

ELIZABETH   *(Stops without turning to look at her)* Yeah?

RUTH   I . . . I'm sorry.

ELIZABETH   You can't be sorry—you're perfect.

(Elizabeth exits. Ruth watches for a moment, sadly, and then exits the other way)

The end.

. . . .

Discussion Questions

1. What's the problem in this sketch? Can you relate to this problem? Why or why not? Have you personally experienced this problem? From whose point of view—Elizabeth's or Ruth's? What was the result?

2. If you were Ruth, how might you help Elizabeth? If you were Elizabeth, how could you deal with your feelings about Ruth and your mother? If you could counsel Elizabeth, Ruth and their mother—what would you advise?

3. Jealousy and rivalry between brothers or sisters isn't a new problem. Read Genesis 27:1-45 (for the outcome read Genesis 33:1-16) and Genesis 37 (for the outcome read Genesis 50:15-21). What practical principles can you glean from these scripture passages? What attitudes are necessary for reconciliation between brothers and sisters? How can you apply these principles to conflict within your own family?

Additional Resources

Also by Chuck Bolte and Paul McCusker:
Youth Ministry Drama & Comedy
(Better Than Bathrobes but Not Quite Broadway)

Also by Chuck Bolte (as editor):
Jeremiah People, Sketch Books: Volumes I-V

Also by Paul McCusker:
Batteries Not Included
The Case of the Frozen Saints
Catacombs
A Family Christmas (with Herb Smith)
Family Outings
The First Church of Pete's Garage
Home for Christmas
The Meaning of Life & Other Vanities (with Tim Albritton)
The Revised Standard Version of Jack Hill
Sketches of Harvest
Souvenirs
Vantage Points
The Waiting Room